D1414462

IT'S UP TO YOU
Language Skills and Strategies for Getting a Job

Mission Language
and
Vocational School
(MLVS)

Joanne Dresner / Kenneth Beck
Clare Morgano / Luise Custer

Longman
New York

IT'S UP TO YOU

Library of Congress Cataloging in Publication Data

Mission Language & Vocational School.
   It's Up to You.

   Accompanied by tape recordings.
   1.   Vocational guidance—Problems, exercises, etc.
2.   Languages and vocational opportunities.
I.   Title.
HF5381.M5548   1980   650.1'4   80-10259
ISBN 0 582 79727 6

First printing 1980

5   4   3   2   1

Sponsoring Editor: Larry Anger
Project Editor: Karen Davy

Designer: Leon Bolognese
Design Assistant: Nilda Scherer
Cover Designer: Dan Serrano

We wish to thank the following artists:
Pages 4 and 5: Anna Veltfort; Page 8: Audrey Sclater; Pages 16, 40, 50, 74 and 93: Nilda Scherer; Pages 37, 38, 53 and 71: Patrick Milbourn.

We also wish to thank the following for providing us with permission to reproduce copyrighted photographs:
Page 18: Monkmeyer Press Photo Service (Mimi Forsyth); Page 25: Photo Researchers, Inc. (Ed Lettau).

The following photographs appear, courtesy of:
Page 13, Top: General Telephone & Electronics Corporation; Center: Texaco (John Keller); Bottom left: Waverly Press, Inc.; Bottom right: AT & T Co.; Page 15: AT & T Co.; Pages 20 and 59: Abe Schrader Corp. (William Plutzer); Page 21: Mayer Hardware, Rochester, New York; Page 24: The Chase Manhattan Bank (Jan Jachniewicz); Page 72: Chemical Bank; Page 81: The Health Insurance Plan of Greater New York (Greene-DeVito).

Special thanks to Mary Greenblatt

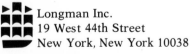 Longman Inc.
19 West 44th Street
New York, New York 10038

Distributed in the United Kingdom by Longman Group Ltd., Longman House, Burnt Mill, Harlow, Essex CM20 2JE, England, and by associated companies, branches and representatives throughout the world.

Printed in the U.S.A.

A WORD FROM MLVS

Mission Language and Vocational School (MLVS) began developing job-related materials in 1962. That year a group of construction workers in San Francisco formed a language center to improve their English in order to compete more effectively for jobs. Since materials for this purpose were non-existent, the laborers and their leaders, supported by other union and community members, worked with volunteer teachers to produce original training materials. With the focus on the vocabulary and communicative skills needed on the job, the program was an immediate success. As the population grew, the center expanded its educational materials and geared new programs to the diverse employment backgrounds of the trainees.

IT'S UP TO YOU is the product of a school which has traditionally stressed responsiveness to the varied needs of the individual student. The school's Education, Student Services and Employment departments work cooperatively to provide comprehensive programs which meet trainees' educational requirements, while helping them nurture the personal and social skills necessary to secure challenging and rewarding employment.

It is deeply satisfying that materials developed with these objectives will now serve a broader population. Because this publication is the work of many individuals, we would like to thank the following: Abel González, and the original MLVS Board of Directors which established the direction of the school; the current Board of Directors whose support made completion of the materials a reality; the members of the Advisory Board; private and public funding agencies; the MLVS staff; the teachers who pilot-tested and critiqued the materials as they were developed; employers of MLVS trainees; and finally, the students whose seriousness of purpose and willingness to cooperate in new projects have been the true motivation of the school and this publication.

José Chapa
Chairman
MLVS Board of Directors

Rosario Anaya
Executive Director

To the Teacher

Many students face the challenge of competing for jobs before they feel proficient in English. IT'S UP TO YOU is a novel approach to developing the language skills and job-seeking strategies of these students. Tapes of actual conversations with job applicants, employees and personnel interviewers were analyzed to isolate the linguistic and social skills important for getting jobs. Excerpts of these conversations accompany this material. They provide models for oral production and examples of sociolinguistic rules that applicants follow, thus recreating a realistic situation in the classroom. They also expose students to natural speech to develop their listening skills.

THE RECORDED CONVERSATIONS should be played as often as necessary until the students fully understand them. To make their listening task easier, they can read the comprehension questions before hearing the cassette. For students having particular difficulty with listening comprehension, the teacher may choose to do some of the follow-up exercises before playing the cassette. Another approach is to summarize the content of the conversation first. (Transcripts of the recorded material can be found at the back of the book.) Once students become familiar with the topics covered in a section, the recording should be easier for them to understand.

VOCABULARY AND FOCUS QUESTIONS introduce each part of Units Two, Five and Six. The vocabulary covers the difficult words used by the speakers in each conversation. The Focus Questions give the students an opportunity to discuss what they already know about a topic and to consider how the topic relates to them. They also help the teacher identify the areas that need to be emphasized for the students. The Focus Questions can also serve as a review at the end of a unit.

UNIT ONE—Before students begin considering specific jobs, it is important for them to be aware of their personal strengths. Regardless of their work experience or training, they have developed attributes, such as dependability or flexibility, that should give them confidence in looking for work. In this unit they explore their reactions to different situations and learn to recognize their strengths. Then they practice talking and writing about themselves in a positive way, in preparation for job interviews.

The vocabulary was selected from actual interviews with employees where they described their successful job performance. Students should not feel that all the vocabulary in an exercise describes them. They should be encouraged to respond honestly when a particular characteristic does not apply to them. (However, the teacher should explain that they should not include negative statements when responding to an interviewer.) At the same time, students need to be reminded that the pairs of words in each exercise are not opposites. They may have both characteristics, even if the words only describe them in some situations.

When the students explain how a trait describes themselves (Part B, 2b of each exercise), the teacher should give any structural guidance they need. They should not be limited to the phrases given as examples. The teacher may also want to present other vocabulary that would help students talk about themselves (such as: attentive, enthusiastic, careful, confident, conscientious, industrious, responsible, etc.).

Every other exercise ends with an interview question. Students choose the vocabulary for which they can give positive supporting information. The teacher should elicit other related vocabulary and encourage students to use any appropriate words to describe themselves positively. At this point it is important for the teacher to indicate what kinds of answers are acceptable for an interview.

UNIT TWO—Applicants often have difficult decisions to make in choosing a job. In this unit students listen to four employees talk about the decisions they had to make.

Part 1—The Hours You Work: Some applicants have to decide if they will take a less desirable work shift to have the job or the pay they want. Jobs in industry, hospitals, restaurants, the post office or computer work often require employees to work different shifts.

Part 2—Job Security: It is important for applicants to consider if they need a job with security. Some factors that affect job security are the stability or the growth potential of a company and the nature of the job (e.g., temporary, seasonal, union protected).

Part 3—Making Decisions: Some people prefer jobs with a lot of responsibility, and others do not. Jobs with responsibility usually require a lot of decision making, but they usually offer better salaries and more status. Jobs without a lot of responsibility usually have less pressure. Students should consider the difference between these two kinds of jobs.

Part 4—Changing Fields: Sometimes applicants have to consider changing fields. For example, they might not have a certificate or license, or there might not be any job openings in their field. Other reasons for changing fields may be better pay or better opportunities to advance. It is a good idea for students to consider a related field that they can turn to.

UNIT THREE—The want ads are a useful vehicle for helping students determine what their qualifications are. By learning to relate their skills, education and experience to specific jobs in the want ads, they should be able to use the information found in most job announcements.

Reading the want ads has been divided into five parts (see the Table of Contents). For each part students have complete want ads to work with. It is not always necessary, however, to read the complete ad to accomplish the objective of an exercise.

Information about job openings is listed differently from ad to ad. An attempt has been made to expose students to some of this variety. For example, punctuation is inconsistent from ad to ad; the kind of information also varies. The abbreviations, however, have generally been limited to one form. The list of abbreviations in Part 2, Exercise 2 represents those that appear throughout IT'S UP TO YOU. There are rules provided in Part 2, Exercise 1 to help students read other abbreviations.

UNIT FOUR—In order to be considered for an interview, applicants need to convince the employer that they meet the requirements of the job. Responding to job announcements by telephone is one way to prepare students to present themselves effectively. While not all students will contact employers by telephone, they may need to present themselves in the same way when making the initial contact in person. Students listen to parts of calls about jobs. The exercises focus their attention on the structures and sociolinguistic rules used.

The Role-play exercises may be done by the teacher playing one role with individual students, by pairs working simultaneously or by pairs demonstrating a role-play for the class. They are most effective when telephone-training equipment is used. This equipment can usually be borrowed from the telephone company.

The last exercise, *A Real Call,* may be done as homework, or it may be taped using a telephone at school. To record a call, a telephone pick-up is attached to a tape recorder. A pick-up can be purchased from a radio and electronics supply store. (The law requires that you inform people that they are being taped.)

UNIT FIVE—Interviewers from many different companies discuss the qualities they look for in job applicants. Students listen to the interviewers talk about the four areas they consider most important.

Part 1—Application Forms: It is often difficult for students to fill out forms well because of the complexity and variety of the instructions. In this unit they practice filling out the most common sections of an application form. Because all aspects of filling out forms are not presented, students may need considerable practice before and/or after this part. The teacher may want to familiarize students with the additional form provided in the Appendix, or with forms from local companies. It is advisable to continue practice in filling out forms over a period of several weeks.

Part 2—Career Goals: Applicants' career goals often indicate their interest in a job and their potential to fit in at a company. While it may be difficult for new applicants to formulate future plans, they need to know that interviewers place a great deal of importance in definite goals. They also need to become familiar with career goals that relate to various jobs, and begin considering their own future plans.

Part 3—Stability: Interviewers look for applicants who have had long-term jobs, good attendance and punctuality, and valid reasons for leaving previous jobs. This usually tells them that applicants will be stable and dependable employees. Thus, it is important for students to learn to present a stable background when they explain their employment history. (For applicants without work experience, their performance in school or what they have done since they left school may indicate to the interviewer their potential stability on a job.)

Part 4—The Questions You Ask: One way for applicants to show interest and assertiveness is by asking good questions at the end of an interview. Examples of the kinds of questions to ask are given. It is important for the teacher to explain the way in which questions should *not* be asked (e.g., "When do I get a raise?" or "When do I get a vacation?").

UNIT SIX—This unit covers four interview questions that many applicants have trouble answering. The questions are difficult because interviewers often have expectations of what a "good" answer would be. Students listen to effective answers, and they also hear answers that illustrate the problems that many applicants have.

For each Role-play exercise, students are asked to take notes on their partner's answers. The teacher should encourage the "applicants" to comment on their own answers first. Then the "interviewers" should offer their comments and suggestions. The teacher should refrain from making any com- ments until both members of the pair being observed have made theirs. It is important for the teacher to stress the importance of the content of the students' answers, and to allow for responses that are not always grammatically perfect.

Part 1—What Can You Tell Me About Yourself?: In response to this open-ended question, it is essential that applicants give information about themselves that is relevant to the job. Personal information should be kept to a minimum.

Part 2—What Are Your Greatest Strengths?: The vocabulary from Unit One should be reviewed before starting this part. When talking about their skills and personal strengths, applicants should always give supporting information from their background.

Part 3—What Do You Consider Your Weaknesses?: The key to answering this question is to avoid sounding negative. To deny having any weaknesses conveys a lack of self-awareness. To state a weakness too candidly can create a negative impression. By mentioning a skill that they need to improve, applicants can be honest and still sound positive.

Part 4—What Are Your Career Goals?: Attaining one's career goals by going to school or by moving up within a company are given as examples. Students should be made aware of other ways to achieve their goals. They could enroll in training programs, study for a licensing exam, attend in-service workshops, etc.

The Symbols Used in IT'S UP TO YOU

●● —Recorded material accompanies the exercise. (There is no recorded material for Units One and Three.)

✳ —The answers can be found in the Answer Key at the back of the book. (Answers for several exercises are provided for teacher reference. For answers to the listening comprehension questions, refer to the Transcript.)

▶ —A "thought" question for discussion, rather than a comprehension question.

Contents

Who Do You Think You Are?

People often have trouble saying good things about themselves. In a job interview, it is important to say why you would be good for the job. You need to think about what makes you a good worker. What things do you do that show you are a good worker? In this unit you will answer questions about yourself and learn to describe your strong points to an interviewer.

Objective: To talk about yourself in a positive way

EXERCISE 1 · HOW DO YOU WORK?

A.

1. What kinds of work do you do around the house, at work and for school?
Make three lists on the blackboard.

2. **Look at the lists on the board.**
   a. Which things do you do fast and which things do you do slowly? Write them.

FAST	SLOWLY
_____	_____
_____	_____
_____	_____
_____	_____

   b. Choose one thing you do fast. Why do you do it fast?
   c. Choose one thing you do slowly. Why do you do it slowly?

3. **Choose the best answer for you, and discuss why you chose it.**

   It is 9 A.M. You are home and have many things to do. You have a doctor's appointment at 11 A.M.
   a. Do you do as many things as you can?
   b. Do you choose one thing and do it completely?
   c. Do you wait until you return from your appointment to begin?

B.

1. **Study the vocabulary below:**
   a. **energetic:** full of energy, active
      —*Energetic* people are usually busy and do a lot of things in a short time.
   b. **thorough:** complete; careful with detail
      —*Thorough* people work carefully and always finish what they begin.

2. **a. Do these words describe you? Check (✔) the correct boxes.**

   YES   NO
   energetic ☐   ☐

   thorough ☐   ☐

   b. Explain your answers.
   FOR EXAMPLE:

   "People say I'm _____ because _____

   _____."

   "It's important for me to be _____ when _____

   _____."

   "Sometimes I'm not _____ when _____

   _____."

EXERCISE 2 · ARE YOU ORGANIZED?

A.

1. **Choose a partner, and ask and answer these questions.**

   What things do you keep . . .

   near your kitchen sink?   in the top of the closet?
   near the telephone?   in the bottom of the closet?
   on the dresser in your bedroom?   under your bed?
   in the top drawer?   in the garage?

2. **Discuss your answers to these questions.**

   a. In what order do you put . . .   **b.** Where do you look for . . .
   the clothes in your closet?   a comb?
   money in your wallet?   a clean piece of paper?
   books on a bookshelf?   a pen?
                                             a cookbook?
                                             an extra set of keys?
                                             your bills?

3. **Choose the best answer for you, and discuss why you chose it.**

   You lost your car keys, and you are looking for an extra set of keys.
   a. You find them immediately.
   b. You find them, but you have to look in several places.
   c. You never find them.

B.

1. **Study the vocabulary below:**

   a. **consistent:** being or acting the same
   —She always leaves the house at 7:45 A.M. and returns at 5:30 P.M.
   She's *consistent*.

   b. **organized:** keeping things in order
   —An *organized* repairman keeps the tools he needs where he can find
   them.

2. **a. Do these words describe you? Check the correct boxes.**

	YES	NO
consistent	☐	☐
organized	☐	☐

   b. Explain your answers.
   FOR EXAMPLE:

   "I like to be _____ because _____

   _____."

   "It's important for me to be _____ when _____

   _____."

   "I don't think I'm _____ because _____

   _____."

3. An employer might ask, "Why do you think you'd be good on the job?"
   Write your answer below. Use the vocabulary you have learned (*energetic, thorough, consistent, organized*) or other words that describe you.

   _____

   _____

   _____

   _____

EXERCISE 3 · ARE YOU FLEXIBLE?
A.
1. **a. Put a check next to the things you sometimes do.**

   take a driving test ☐
   clean the house ☐
   pay bills ☐
   do homework ☐
   shop for groceries ☐
   wash the car ☐
   write letters ☐

   b. What other things do you sometimes do? _____

   _____

   _____

2. **Use the list above and complete these sentences.**

   a. I need to concentrate ¹ when I _____

   _____

   _____

   b. I don't need to concentrate when I _____

   _____

   _____

3. **Choose the best answers for you, and discuss why you chose them.**

   a. You are painting the bathroom, and your brother and sister come to visit.
   1. Do you talk with them and finish painting?
   2. Do you stop painting and finish when they leave?
   3. Do you stop painting and not return to it for a long time?

   b. You are studying for a test, and you need to concentrate. Someone asks you a few questions. How do you feel?
   Angry? ☐
   Nervous? ☐
   Calm? ☐

---

¹ concentrate: give complete attention to

B.

1. **Study the vocabulary below:**

   a. **disciplined:**   using control and order in one's actions
      —*Disciplined* students do their work on time and study when they should.

   b. **flexible:**   able to change to a new situation
      —Secretaries have to be *flexible* to answer the phone while they're typing.

2. **a. Do these words describe you? Check the correct boxes.**

	YES	NO
disciplined	☐	☐
flexible	☐	☐

   b. Explain your answers.
   FOR EXAMPLE:

   "People say I'm _____ because _____

   _____."

   "I need to be _____ when _____

   _____."

   "It's hard for me to be _____ when _____

   _____."

EXERCISE 4 · ARE YOU COOPERATIVE?

A.

1. **Discuss your answers to these questions.**

   a. Do you like helping other people . . .

   paint their house?   prepare for a party?
   move into a new home?   buy clothes?
   fix a car?

   b. How do you feel when people ask you for help? (happy? angry? nervous?)

2. **Choose the best answers for you, and discuss why you chose them.**

   a. You are a file clerk in an office. A secretary asks you to help her. She asks you to take things to other offices and do some typing. You also have to do your own work.

   1. Are you happy to help the secretary?
   2. Are you angry about the extra work?
   3. Are you nervous that you won't be able to do the extra work and also finish your own work?

   b. You have a lot of work to do, and you must finish by the end of the day.
   1. Do you ask someone to help you?
   2. Do you work by yourself?

B.

1. **Study the vocabulary below:**

   a. **cooperative:**   helpful; able to work well with other people
   —He's not *cooperative* because he never helps clean up the office.

   b. **independent:**   not needing other people or things; able to work well alone
   —She's *independent*. She prefers to work by herself and doesn't like to
   ask other people for help.

2. **a. Do these words describe you? Check the correct boxes.**

   YES   NO

   cooperative   ☐   ☐

   independent   ☐   ☐

   b. Explain your answers.
   FOR EXAMPLE:

   "I'm a(n) _____ person. I prefer to _____

   _____."

   "I think I'm _____ because _____

   _____."

3. An employer might ask, "Do you prefer to work with others or to work alone?"

   **Write your answers below. Use the vocabulary you have learned (*disciplined*, *flexible*,
   independent, *cooperative*) or other words that describe you.**

   _____

   _____

   _____

   _____

   _____

   _____

EXERCISE 5 · ARE YOU DEPENDABLE?

A.

1. **a. Check the things you are usually early for, on time for or late for.**

	EARLY	ON TIME	LATE
doctor's appointment			
party			
dinner at a friend's house			
job interview			
airport			
appointment with a friend			

   b. Discuss your answers above. Talk about the difference between business and social appointments. Should you be early for some appointments? Can you be late for some appointments?

2. **Choose the best answer for you, and discuss why you chose it.**

You told some friends that you would meet them for a picnic. Then your friend John calls from the airport and asks you to pick him up.
   a. Do you tell John that you can't pick him up?
   b. Do you pick John up at the airport and explain to your other friends later?

3. You have an appointment with a friend. He (or she) arrives forty-five minutes late. How does this make you feel? What do you say?

B.

1. **Study the vocabulary below:**

   a. **dependable:**   doing what should be done
                     —He always finishes his work and does a good job. He's *dependable*.

   b. **patient:**   relaxed when things are slow or difficult
                     —She didn't get angry when the bus was late. She was *patient* and read the newspaper while she waited.

2. **a. Do these words describe you? Check the correct boxes.**

               YES   NO
   dependable ☐ ☐

   patient   ☐ ☐

   b. Explain your answers.
   FOR EXAMPLE:

   "People say I'm _____ because _____

   _____."

   "I need to be _____ when _____

   _____."

   "Sometimes I'm not _____ when _____

   _____."

EXERCISE 6 · ARE YOU ASSERTIVE?

A.

1. **Read this situation:**

   You are renting an apartment. There are many things that are broken. You talk to the owner and give him a list of the things that are broken. He can only fix three of them this month. You have to choose the three that are the most important.

   a. In small groups (four or five people), look at the picture and choose only three things that are important to all of you.

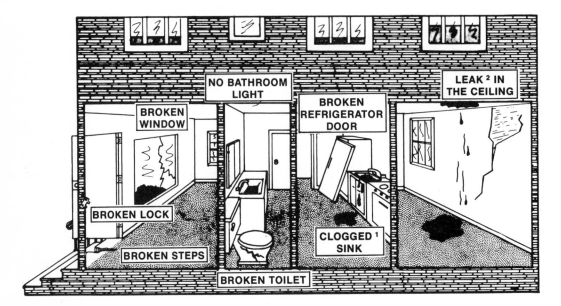

   b. Discuss with the class the three things your group chose. Explain why you chose them.

   c. Discuss these questions:
   1. In your small groups, did anyone become the leader?
   2. Did some people talk more than others?
   3. Which people felt the strongest about what to choose?

2. **Choose the best answers for you, and discuss why you chose them.**

   a. You are with a group of friends who want to see a movie. The movie doesn't interest you at all. You want to go to a museum.
   1. Will you try to talk your friends into going to a museum?
   2. Will you go to the movie with them?
   3. Will you go to a museum by yourself?

   b. You are in class, and you don't understand an exercise.
   1. Will you ask a question?
   2. Will you try to do the exercise without understanding it completely?

---

[1] clogged: stopped (the water will not go down)

[2] leak: small hole (water comes through)

B.

1. **Study the vocabulary below:**

    a. **assertive:**   direct, not shy or timid
                                  —She's an *assertive* person.When there's a problem in the office, she tries to do something about it.

    b. **to get along well**
       with others: to be friendly and cooperative
                                  —Many different kinds of people work at his company. He *gets along well with* all of them.

2. **a. Do these words describe you? Check the correct boxes.**

                           YES   NO

    assertive   ☐   ☐

    **get along well
    with others**   ☐   ☐

    b. Explain your answers.
    FOR EXAMPLE:

    "In most situations I ('m) _____. I usually _____

    _____."

    "It's important to (be) _____ because _____

    _____."

    "It's hard for me to (be) _____ when _____

    _____."

3. An employer might ask, "How would you describe yourself?"

    Write your answer below. Use the vocabulary you have learned (*dependable, patient, assertive, get along well with others*) or other words that describe you.

_____

_____

_____

_____

EXERCISE 7 · VOCABULARY REVIEW

Read the sentences below and fill in the blanks with the correct answers.

1. He's a _____ person. He's always careful to complete his work.
   a. thorough
   b. patient

2. They're very _____. They're hard workers, and they work quickly.
   a. assertive
   b. energetic

3. She's an _____ person. She plans the things she does, and she keeps
   them in order.
   a. organized
   b. independent

4. I'm very _____. I enjoy doing different kinds of things, and I can
   move easily from one thing to another.
   a. consistent
   b. flexible

5. People say that he's _____. He likes working with other people.
   a. disciplined
   b. cooperative

6. She _____. When she says she'll do something, she always does it.
   a. is dependable
   b. gets along well with others

7. I'm a _____ person. I stay calm when things get difficult.
   a. patient
   b. dependable

8. People say he's a _____ person. He does his work, even when he's
   tired.
   a. flexible
   b. disciplined

▶Which sentences above describe you?

EXERCISE 8 · TALKING TO THE INTERVIEWER

A.

**Here are some questions that an interviewer might ask. Circle the best answer for each.
Why would you *not* give the other answers?**

1. **Interviewer:** Why do you think you'd be good on the job?

   You: _____

   a. I'm organized and thorough. I plan my work carefully, and I like to finish things.
   b. I'm organized and thorough. I think I'm a good worker.

2. **Interviewer:** Do you like to work with others, or by yourself?

   You: _____

   a. I usually like to work with others, but I also work well by myself.
   b. I like to work with others. I don't like to work by myself.

3. **Interviewer:** How would you describe yourself?

   You: _____

   a. I'm energetic and flexible. I don't like to do the same thing all the time.
   b. I'm energetic and flexible. I like to keep busy and do a lot of different things.

B.
Look at the list below. Next to the words that describe you, write a sentence to explain why.
FOR EXAMPLE:

dependable _I'm seldom absent, and I always finish my work on time._

1. assertive _____

2. consistent _____

3. cooperative _____

4. dependable _____

5. disciplined _____

6. energetic _____

7. flexible _____

8. get along well with others _____

_____

9. independent _____

10. organized _____

11. patient _____

12. thorough _____

People choose jobs for different reasons. In this unit you will hear four employees talk about why they chose their jobs. As you listen, think about what is important to you when you choose a job.

What Do You Think You'll Do?

Part 1

THE HOURS YOU WORK

Objective: To consider the different hours you might work, and why

INTRODUCTION

Before you listen to the recording, study the vocabulary below. Then discuss the Focus Questions.

VOCABULARY

1. **be trained for:**   prepare for a specific kind of work
                                —He *was trained for* sales work.

2. **eventually:**   after a certain amount of time
                                —Some store clerks *eventually* become managers.

3. **field:**   a general area of work
                                —Doctors and nurses work in the medical *field*.
                                Receptionists and secretaries work in the clerical *field*.

4. **keypunch operator:**   a person who types information onto cards to be used by computers
                                —If you want to work with computers, you usually start as a *keypunch operator*.

5. **move up:**   change to a better job in the company
                                —When you *move up*, you usually have more work to do. You also make more money.

6. **offer:**   ask someone if he or she wants something
                                —They *offered* me the job, but I said no.

7. **prefer:**   like better
                                —Most employers *prefer* to hire people who learn quickly.

8. **shift:**   a work period that is usually eight hours
                                —The day *shift* is usually from 9 A.M. to 5 P.M.

Focus Questions

A. What is more important to you—the kind of work you do, or the hours you work?

B. Are there certain hours you would not work?

EXERCISE 1

You will now hear a conversation with Mark Kendall, a keypunch operator. He works for the telephone company from 4:00 in the afternoon to 12:30 at night.

Listen to the recording. Then answer the questions.

1. Why does Mark work nights?

2. How does he like working nights?

3. He was offered an office job during the day. Why didn't he take it?

 Would you work nights to have the job you wanted?

EXERCISE 2

Role-Play: Interviewer and Applicant

Different kinds of work have different shifts.

Look at the shifts listed below.

> **THE DAY SHIFT IS GENERALLY FROM 9:00 A.M. TO 5:00 P.M.**
>
> **THE AFTERNOON SHIFT[1] IS GENERALLY FROM 12:00 P.M. TO 8:00 P.M.**
>
> **THE NIGHT SHIFT[2] IS GENERALLY FROM 12:00 A.M. TO 8:00 A.M.**

For some jobs you have to be able to work when the company needs you.

Choose a partner and practice asking and answering the interview question: "Can you work the _____ shift?"

FOR EXAMPLE:

INTERVIEWER   APPLICANT

"Can you work the *afternoon* shift?"   "Yes. In fact,[3] I like to work *afternoons*."
                                                          or
                                             "No, I'm sorry.[4] I can't work *afternoons*."

1. "_____ the day shift?"   1. "_____"

2. "_____ the afternoon   2. "_____"
    shift?"

3. "_____ the night shift?"   3. "_____"

---

[1] afternoon shift: sometimes called the "swing shift"

[2] night shift: sometimes called the "graveyard shift"

[3] "In fact" is often used before you give more information.

[4] "I'm sorry" is often used to say "no" in a polite way.

Part 2

JOB SECURITY

Objective: To consider if job security is important to you

INTRODUCTION

Before you listen to the recording, study the vocabulary below. Then discuss the Focus Questions.

VOCABULARY

1. **apply:**   ask for
             —He wants to *apply* for a job in the medical field.

2. **benefits:**   the extra things that go with a job, such as health insurance, sick leave, vacation time
             —Medical *benefits* save employees money when they are sick.

3. **electronics:**   a field of work related to electricity
             —People who design computers have studied *electronics*.

4. **hire:**   give a job to
             —They *hired* four new bank tellers last week.

5. **job security:** knowing that a job will probably continue for a long time
             —A large, successful company usually offers good *job security*.

6. **salary:**   the money a person gets for his or her work
             —He changed jobs because he was offered a better *salary*.

7. **welder:**   a person who puts metal parts together by heating them
             —*Welders* are needed to build things like ships and cars.

Focus Questions

A. How do you know if a job has security?

B. Is job security important to you? Is it more important to you than the kind of work you do?

EXERCISE 1

You will now hear a conversation with Pat Hanes, a welder. She studied welding for one year, and now she works for an electronics company.

Listen to the recording. Then answer the questions.

1. Why did Pat accept this job?

2. Why didn't she take the job with a better salary?

▶ Why do you think some people want job security?

EXERCISE 2

Some jobs have more security than others.

Read about the four jobs below. Then answer the questions.

1. Rita Wong is a bookkeeper. She is working for an automobile company while the regular bookkeeper is going to school. The job is for one year.
   a. What will she have to do at the end of the year?
   b. Does this job have security?

2. Charlie Sullivan lives in Michigan. He paints houses during good weather (from April to October) every year.
   a. What does Charlie have to do at the end of October?
   b. Would you like this kind of work? Why or why not?

3. Michael Simon is an insurance salesman. The company he works for is getting bigger. They are hiring more people every year. Most of the employees have worked there for several years, and many have moved up to better jobs.
   a. Do you think this job has security?
   b. Would you like to work for a company like this? Why or why not?

4. Lynn Yamada is a teacher. She teaches in a special program that the government set up for one year. The program will end if the government does not give more money for another year.
   a. What will Lynn have to do if the program ends?
   b. Would you take a job like this? Why or why not?

Part 3
MAKING DECISIONS

Objective: To consider how much responsibility you want on a job

INTRODUCTION

Before you listen to the recording, study the vocabulary below. Then discuss the Focus Questions.

VOCABULARY

1. **be responsible for:**   have a specific job to do
   —A waitress *is responsible for* bringing the food to the table.

2. **break down:**   stop working
   —We couldn't use the machine because it *broke down.*

3. **in good working order:**   working well
   —The employees kept their adding machines *in good working order.*

4. **make a decision:**   choose what to do
   —The company offered him two different jobs. He has to *make a decision* about which job he wants.

5. **maintenance:**   the job of keeping things in good working order
   —He is responsible for the *maintenance* of all the machines.

6. **repair:**   fix
   —An auto mechanic *repairs* cars.

7. **responsibility:**   something or someone to take care of
   —The last person to leave the building has the *responsibility* to lock the doors.

8. **take a chance:**   do something you are not sure about, but you hope that it is right
   —You *take a chance* when you buy a used car.

Focus Questions

A. Do you have to make a lot of decisions at home? What kinds of decisions do you make?

B. How do you feel when you have a lot of responsibility?

C. Think about the jobs that interest you. Do you have to make more decisions on some jobs than on others?

EXERCISE 1

You will now hear a conversation with Joseph Panos. He worked for several years repairing cars. Now he works as a maintenance man at a clothing factory.

Listen to the recording. Then answer the questions.

1. How is his new job different from his last job?

2. Why was he comfortable on his last job?

▶ Joseph took a chance when he changed jobs. Do you think he has a better job now than he had before? Why or why not?

EXERCISE 2

You have to make more decisions on some jobs than you do on other jobs.

FOR EXAMPLE:

> A person who plans the work makes more decisions than a person who follows the plans.
>
> A person who gives instructions makes more decisions than a person who follows instructions.

Joseph Panos decided to take a job in which he has to make a lot of decisions. Not everyone would accept that kind of job.

Now read about Arthur Zeller and answer the questions.

Arthur Zeller is a salesman in a hardware store. He helps customers find things, answers questions and works at the cash register. His boss asked him to be the manager of one of the departments. Managers are responsible for the whole department. They decide what to order, plan the hours and jobs of the other employees and report sales to the store manager. Sometimes they have to work longer hours. They also make more money.

Arthur decided not to take the job. He does not want to have more responsibility, and he prefers not to work longer hours.

1. What is the difference between the salesman's job and the manager's job?

2. What do you think of Arthur's reasons for not taking the manager's job?

3. How can he tell his boss he does not want the job?

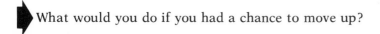 What would you do if you had a chance to move up?

EXERCISE 3

A. Discuss which person makes more decisions:

1. The person who tells someone what to type, or the person who types?
2. The person who buys paper for the office, or the person who plans how much paper to buy?
3. The person who decides the prices of things, or the person who tells the customer how much to pay?
4. The person who files the cards, or the person who says how to file them?

B. Compare two different jobs in the same field.

1. Read the job duties [1] below. Which duties does a waitress usually have? Which duties does a restaurant manager usually have? Write the duties under the correct job title.

—sets the tables   —plans the workers' hours
—takes food orders   —brings the food to the table
—directs the work in the dining room   —talks to customers about problems

A WAITRESS	**A RESTAURANT MANAGER**
_____	_____
_____	_____
	_____

Which person makes more decisions? _____

2. Look at the job duties of an auto mechanic and a service station attendant. Write the duties under the correct job title.

—fixes motors   —decides what to repair
—checks the oil   —pumps gas
—washes the car windows   —buys automobile parts

AN AUTO MECHANIC	**A SERVICE STATION ATTENDANT**
_____	_____
_____	_____
_____	_____

Which person makes more decisions? _____

3. Below are the job duties of a secretary and a file clerk. Write the duties under the correct job title.

—puts folders in alphabetical and   —pulls folders from the files
   numerical order   —puts labels on folders
—writes and types letters   —organizes the work of the file clerk
—makes appointments

A SECRETARY	**A FILE CLERK**
_____	_____
_____	_____
_____	_____

Which person makes more decisions? _____

---

[1] job duties: the different kinds of work a person does on a job

Part 4
CHANGING FIELDS

Objective: To consider when it is necessary to change fields

INTRODUCTION

Before you listen to the recording, study the vocabulary below. Then discuss the Focus Questions.

VOCABULARY

1. **career:**   the kind of work you plan to do for a long time
   —He studied welding for two years. Then he began his *career* as a welder.

2. **certificate:**   a paper that says a person knows how to do a job
   —Most teachers need a *certificate* to get a teaching job.

3. **entry level:**   beginning level
   —Keypunch is an *entry-level* job for working with computers.

4. **realize:**   understand clearly
   —After thinking about the problem, he *realized* his mistakes.

5. **temporary:**   for a short time
   —She had a *temporary* job for two weeks.

Focus Questions

A. If you can't find work in the field you want, what other kind of work might interest you?

B. What kind of work would you never want to do?

EXERCISE 1

You will now hear a conversation with Francisco Pérez, a clerical worker at a bank.

Listen to the recording. Then answer the questions.

1. What did Francisco do in Colombia?

2. Why couldn't he get a teaching job?

3. Why did he decide to take a job in a bank?

Francisco decided to change careers. Do you think he made a good decision?

EXERCISE 2

Read the situations below. Choose the job that you think each person should apply for. Discuss your answers. All of the answers can be correct.

1. Ana Nasir is a nurse's aide.[1] She moved with her family to a small town where there are no job openings for a nurse's aide. She should look for a job as a:
   - a. child care worker.
   - b. file clerk at a hospital.
   - c. cafeteria manager.

2. Ursula Schmidt was an accountant [2] in Germany. She needs a certificate to work as an accountant in the United States. She doesn't want to study for the certificate. She should apply for a job as a:
   - a. cashier.
   - b. secretary.
   - c. small store manager.

3. Peter Thompson is an electrician.[3] He is on a waiting list to join an electrician's union. The union says it may be two years before he can join. He should apply for a job as a (n):
   - a. auto mechanic.
   - b. typewriter repairman.
   - c. TV-stereo salesman.

4. Henry Chin was a lawyer in Taiwan. He can't work as a lawyer in the United States until he passes a state examination. He needs a job now. He should apply for a job as a :
   - a. salesman.
   - b. bilingual classroom aide.
   - c. general office clerk.

---

[1] aide: helper

[2] accountant: a person who is responsible for the money records of a business

[3] electrician: a person who works with electricity

What Will You Find Out?

The newspaper is one place to look for job openings. In this unit you will learn how to use information about jobs to help you decide what to apply for. You will also learn what to do before contacting the companies you are interested in.

Part 1

AN INTRODUCTION TO THE WANT ADS

Objective: To find the job announcements you are looking for in the want ads

EXERCISE 1 · LOOKING IN THE RIGHT PLACE

Newspapers have advertisements for jobs. They are in a section called the *classified ads*.[1] Another name for the classified ads is the "want ads."

There are several kinds of want ads for jobs. *Jobs Wanted* and *Help Wanted* are two important kinds.

Look at the want ads below. When you look for a job, where do you look? Circle JOBS WANTED or HELP WANTED.

JOBS WANTED

ACCOUNTANT—has experience, can work 8–1 756-8004.

BABYSITTER
Daily, will come to your house. Call 474-6789 Sue.

KEYPUNCH OPERATOR can work any shift. Fast, dependable. Jane Roberts 642-3881

NURSE'S AIDE. Needs work immediately. Call 387-5153.

PAINTER—summers only 285-8175

TUTOR Math in your home 776-1359

TYPIST
Will type papers for students. $1.00 a page. Neat. 211-6800.

HELP WANTED

ACCOUNTANT—a large company is looking for several accountants with 2–4 years' experience (313) 365-4646

AIRLINE—needs office workers. Apply in person. 755 Brown St.

BANK TELLER—Must have 1 year's experience—National Bank 678-3425.

BARTENDER
Weekends only Holiday House 382-4445

BOOKKEEPER[2] male/female 6 months' experience 567-4523.

CARPENTER—w/gen. bldg. skills. Must have own tools and trans. 771-2433 ext. 18

---

[1] ads: advertisements

[2] bookkeeper: the person who writes down information about the money of a business

EXERCISE 2 · FINDING A SPECIFIC JOB

Look at the want ads in Exercise 1. Are they in a special order?

Newspapers list want ads in alphabetical order. The following want ads are not in the right order.

Write the job titles [1] in alphabetical order on the lines below.

SECRETARY. Small office. San Francisco. Pat. 873-2404	**OFFICE CLERK**—must be flexible. 952-9658
MECHANIC For trucks. Must have experience, write to P.O. Box 281, Shady Cove, Ore. 95739	**RECEPTIONIST**—hospital. Experienced, 5-day wk., write this paper. Ad. 27954
AUTO PAINTER—experienced only. 861-7992	**TYPIST**—70 words a minute, 4 hrs. daily 362-7627
HAIRSTYLIST—Murray Hill Salon 711-5500	**CLERK-TYPIST**—part time [3] 1 yr. office experience, 25 hrs. per wk. 781-2930
MEDICAL SECRETARY Full time,[2] top salary job. Typing. 922-1311	**GUARDS**—Good pay and vacations. Apply 768 Brannan St., Salinas
BARTENDER—Napa Restaurants 282-9547 10–3 P.M.	**SHIPPING CLERK** Good handwriting, good with numbers. Call Mr. Adams at 529-9300.

1. _____   7. _____
2. _____   8. _____
3. _____   9. _____
4. _____   10. _____
5. _____   11. _____
6. _____   12. _____

[1] job titles: names of jobs

[2] full time: usually forty hours of work a week

[3] part time: less than full time

Part 2
WANT AD ABBREVIATIONS
Objective: To read abbreviations

EXERCISE 1 · HOW ABBREVIATIONS ARE WRITTEN

Abbreviations are short forms of words. They are written in different ways. The following rules will help you read abbreviations in want ads.

Rule 1: Many abbreviations use the first few letters of words.

mach. = *mach*ine
sal. = *sal*ary
gen. = *gen*eral

Can you guess what these abbreviations mean?

betw. = _____
co. = _____
typ. = _____

Rule 2: Some abbreviations use the first letters and the last letters of words.

wk. = *w*ee*k*
lge. = *l*ar*ge*
appt. = *app*ointmen*t*

Can you guess what these abbreviations mean?

hr. = _____
yr. = _____
dept. = _____

Rule 3: Some abbreviations leave out the vowels and some consonants.

bldg. = *bldg*
mgr. = *m*ana*ger*

Can you guess what these abbreviations mean?

dwntwn. = _____
bkkpr. = _____

Rule 4: Some abbreviations use the first letter of each word. Sometimes these abbreviations have a slash (/).

f/t	=	*full time*
w/	=	*with*
EOE	=	*Equal Opportunity Employer* [1]

Can you guess what these abbreviations mean?

| p/t | = | _____ |
| wpm | = | _____ [2] |

Rule 5: A few abbreviations use more than one rule.

secty.   =   *secretary*

Can you guess what this abbreviation means?

ofc.   =   _____

 Why do you think abbreviations are used in want ads?

EXERCISE 2 · READING ABBREVIATIONS

A.
Look at the want ads below. Try to think of the meaning of each abbreviation. Then write the complete word next to the abbreviation.

FOR EXAMPLE:

> **HANDYMAN**—m/f. min. 5 yrs. exp., good salary. Call 771-4585

m/f = *male/female*
min. = *minimum*
yrs. = *years*
exp. = *experience*

AD #1

> **SECRETARY FOR SHIPPING[3] CO.** good typ. good w/numbers. Write P.O. Box 47, Detroit, Michigan

co. = _____
typ. = _____
w/   = _____
P.O. = _____

AD #2

> **AUTO MECHANIC**—Must have exp. with foreign cars, hrs. 8–5 850 Maine St., Salinas EOE

exp. = _____
hrs. = _____
St. = _____
EOE = _____

---

[1] Equal Opportunity Employer: an employer that gives jobs to people of any age, sex or race

[2] wpm: how many words a person types in one minute

[3] shipping: sending and receiving things

B.
The abbreviations below are often used in the want ads. The full words are written next to some of them. Write the full words for the other abbreviations. Use the list on the right to help you.

1. accnt. _____

2. accntg. *accounting* (the field of work of an accountant)

3. accur. *accurate* (with no mistakes)

4. apt. _____

5. appt. _____

6. asst. *assistant* (a helper)

7. ben. _____

8. betw. _____

9. bkkpr. _____

10. bldg. _____

11. co. _____

12. dept. _____

13. dwntwn. _____

14. elec. *electrician*
    OR *electronics*

15. EOE _____
    _____

16. equip. *equipment* (the things a person uses on a job)

17. exc. _____

18. exp. *experience*
    OR *experienced*

19. ext. *extension* (one of the many telephones that have the same telephone number)

20. fig. *figures* (numbers)

21. F/T _____

22. gd. _____

23. gen. _____

24. hr. _____

25. hrs. _____

apartment

department

hours

appointment

hour

benefits

general

accountant

excellent

full time

Equal Opportunity
Employer

downtown

company

good

building

bookkeeper

between

26. H.S. grad. _high_   (a person who finished high school)
school graduate

27. lge. _____

28. lt, lite _light_   (not very much [work])

29. mach. _____

30. maint. _____

31. m/f _____

32. mgr. _____

33. min. _minimum_   (the smallest number of something
                    that a person needs)

34. M-F _monday_
through Friday

35. mo. _____

36. ofc. _____

37. oppty. _opportunity_ (a good chance)

38. P/T _____

39. perm. _permanent_ (for a long time)

40. pref. _prefer_
or preferred

41. prev. _previous_ (before)

42. qual. _qualified_ (having ability and knowledge
                    for a specific job)

OR _qualifications_ (ability and knowledge)

43. req. _require_   (need)
OR _required_   (needed)

44. sal. _____

45. secty. _____

46. s/h _shorthand_ (a fast way of writing)

47. sm. _____

48. trans. _transportation_ (how you go from one place to
                    another)

49. vac. _____

50. wk. _____

51. w/_____

52. wpm _____

_____

53. yr. _____

54. yrs. _____

office

secretary

large

month

part time

year

small

machine

salary

male or female

manager

years

words per minute

vacation

with

week

maintenance

Part 3

THE INFORMATION IN AN AD

Objective: To find job requirements, preferred qualifications and information about a job in a want ad

EXERCISE 1 · JOB REQUIREMENTS

Requirements are the skills,[1] knowledge, experience and other things you must have to get a job. For example, to get some jobs, you must be a high school graduate. For other jobs you must type 50 words a minute.

Words like *must, required (req.)* or *minimum (min.)* will often help you find the requirements. But some ads give requirements without these words.

Underline the requirements in the ads below.

FOR EXAMPLE:

> **CASHIER:** Full Time. 24-hr. station. <u>Min. requirements—must be 18 yrs. of age, have own transportation, h.s. grad.</u> Apply in person, 420 Van St., Houston EOE

1.
> **APT. MANAGER** —some maintenance exp. required,[2] and own trans. 398-7091

2.
> **BOOKKEEPER**
> Experience req. Must have good knowledge of 10-key adding mach., type 55 wpm. Apply at Tracy's Dept. Store 170 O'Farrell
> An equal opportunity employer

3.
> **GEN. OFC. CLERK**
> Good typing, filing for small office 421-2272

---

[1] skills: things you know how to do (type, speak another language)

[2] Exp. required: "Experience *is* required"

EXERCISE 2 · PREFERRED QUALIFICATIONS

Preferred qualifications are the skills, knowledge, experience and other things that employers would like applicants to have. They are not necessary to have, but they help you get the job.

Words like *prefer* (*pref.*), *desired* and *helpful* will help you find the preferred qualifications.

Underline the preferred qualifications in the ads below.

FOR EXAMPLE:

> **CLERK**—Gen. ofc. work. —mail & filing, sm. insur- ance office. <u>Prefer some work exp.</u> Must type 40–45. Call Pamela 421-1103

1.
> **MAINTENANCE WORK** Must have car, pref. own tools.[1] 751 Larkin Blvd. 775-9101

2.
> **MACHINE OPERATOR**— must have mechanical ability. Prev. exp. desired.[2] Call Ted 642-1131

3.
> **RECEPTIONIST/GENERAL OFFICE** Phone, typing. Hospital exp. helpful. Call 567- 2967 for appt.

---

[1] tools: things you hold in your hands to do a job (hammer, saw)

[2] Prev. exp. desired: "Previous experience *is* desired."

EXERCISE 3 · INFORMATION ABOUT THE JOB

Information about the job tells about the company or office, the job duties, the salary or wage,[1] the hours, the benefits and the opportunities.[2] It also tells if the job is full time or part time. This information can help you decide if you want the job.

The information about the job is underlined in the ads below. Check what kind of information about the job is in each ad.

	TYPE OF CO.	F/T or P/T	DUTIES	SALARY OR WAGE	HOURS	BENEFITS	OPPORTUNITIES
FOR EXAMPLE: **ELECTRONICS ASST.** <u>TV & Stereo Co. Part time,</u> <u>Exc. salary. Hours Mon.–Fri. 1–6.</u> 457-1007	✓	✓		✓	✓		
1. **SERVICE STATION AT-TENDANT** Exp. req. <u>Full time $3.25/hr. night shift.</u> Shell-corner Fell & Baker.							
2. **RECEPTIONIST** for <u>den-tal ofc. 4-day wk. answer phones, good benefits.</u> Write to this paper, Ad no. 17294.							
3. **ACCOUNTING CLERK** for <u>small insurance office. Exp. pref.[3] Gd. salary. Room to ad-vance[4]</u> 435-0946							

---

[1] wage: the money a person gets for one hour of work

[2] opportunities: chances to move up

[3] Exp. pref.: "Experience is preferred."

[4] room to advance: opportunity to move up

EXERCISE 4 · LOOKING FOR DIFFERENT KINDS OF INFORMATION

✳

Can you separate the requirements, preferred qualifications and information about the job in a want ad? If you can, this will help you decide which jobs to apply for.

Make notes of the important information. Try to abbreviate when you write the information.

FOR EXAMPLE:	INFORMATION ABOUT JOB	REQUIREMENTS	PREFERRED QUALIFICATIONS
CASHIER—Full time with good salary and benefits. High school graduate. Typing and cashiering experience preferred. Call 624-1851, ext. 292	*F/T* *gd. sal. + ben.*	*h.s. grad.*	*typ. + cashier exp.*

1.

CLERK TYPIST M/F for airlines. Must be able to type 65 wpm accurately and work afternoon shift. 1 yr. clerical exper. Call 788-8100, ext. 225			

2.

MACHINE REPAIR Must have exp., electrical knowledge preferred. Sm. TV-Stereo company 14 Mile Road. Call Barbara 585-8220 for appt.			

3.

MAINTENANCE MECHANIC Must have exp. in repair of equip., work in electrical repair pref. Must have own hand tools. Sheldon Transport Company, 17011 Beaumont, Salt Lake City, Utah 84112			

4.

MECHANIC—exp. in bldg. repairs. Knowledge of elec. tools helpful, gd. sal. & ben. Engineering company 52 First St., Cambridge 547-2700			

	INFORMATION ABOUT JOB	REQUIREMENTS	PREFERRED QUALIFICATIONS

5.

OFFICE MGR. for doctor's office. Bilingual Spanish/English. Good telephone manner.[1] 8–5 P.M. 648-6066.

6.

PAINTERS HELPER wanted.[2] No exp. required. Start $4.30 hr. 960-8614

7.

RECEPTIONIST Answer busy phones, meet public, type letters, other office duties. Good phone manner and typing required. Min. 1 year office exper. Good salary & benefits. CITY SAVINGS & LOAN 700 Market St. 772-1481.

8.

SECRETARY—full time, 10–6 M–F. Must type 65 wpm. Some office exp. preferred. Ask for Susan 527-8047

9.

SERVICE STATION Attendant—1 yr. exper. 5 days 40 hrs. Tues–Sat. Apply at Union Oil, 300 W. Portal Ave. San Francisco

10.

WELDER Move to beautiful Vermont. Good benefits & working cond. Min. 5 yrs. exp. Call 802 689-5034 or write to Route 1, Brattleboro, Vt. 05301

---

[1] manner: way of doing something

[2] Painters helper wanted: "A painter's helper is wanted." (Ads do not always use apostrophes ['].)

Part 4

YOUR QUALIFICATIONS

Objective: To relate your qualifications to the requirements of a job

EXERCISE 1 · QUALIFICATIONS AND JOB REQUIREMENTS

Qualifications include work experience, education and skills.

When you apply for a job, think about your experience on past jobs, your education and your skills. Do they relate [1] to the requirements of the job?

A. Read about this person's qualifications.

Tina Taylor is applying for a job as a secretary. She worked as a waitress when she was in high school. Then she worked in an office for two years. She can type 65 words a minute, and she can take dictation at 100 words a minute.

Read the ad. Then read Tina's qualifications next to the ad. She listed them to get ready to apply for the job.

> **SECTY**—Electronics Co. needs secty. for president. Typing 60 wpm., s/h 100 wpm. Call 552-1247 for appt.

typ. 65 wpm
s/h 100 wpm
2 yrs. ofc. exp.

Now answer these questions.

1. Does Tina have the qualifications for the job?

2. Why does she list her office experience?

3. Why doesn't she list her experience as a waitress?

---

[1] Do they relate?: "Are they similar?"

B. Read about this person's qualifications.

Mario Vanessi is applying for a job as a maintenance man. He worked as a plumber [1] for two years. He studied carpentry [2] at night school last year. He has been working part time building kitchen cabinets for the last six months.

Read the ad. Then read Mario's qualifications next to the ad.

MAINTENANCE PERSON
P/T for lge. apt. bldg. Responsible for gen. maintenance & repairs. Must have own tools. Write to P.O. Box 1788, Phoenix, Az. 85282

plumber- 2 yrs. exp.
carpentry class
own tools
cabinet work - 6 mos.

Now answer these questions.

1. Does Mario have the qualifications for the job?

2. Does the carpentry class relate to maintenance and repairs?

3. Why does he list his part-time job building cabinets?

---

[1] plumber: a person who works with water and gas pipes

[2] carpentry: the field of building things with wood

EXERCISE 2 · RELATING YOUR QUALIFICATIONS

Look at the want ads in your local newspaper. Choose two jobs you would like to apply for. Underline the requirements and preferred qualifications. Then list your qualifications for each ad.

FOR EXAMPLE:

Ex. #1   HAL'S QUALIFICATIONS

> **BANK TELLER**
> 30-hr. wk. Previous banking exper. & lt. typing req. Apply in person—First California Bank, 49 El Camino Real, San Diego EOE

6 mos. teller exp.
type 40 wpm
ofc. work - 1 yr. exp.

Ex. #2   ANGELA'S QUALIFICATIONS

> **ELECTRICIAN** m/f, night shift. Must have own tools and exp. w/large motors, gd. benefits $8.15/hr. Call 632-3467 Miami Beach EOE

own tools
lge. motors - 2 yrs. exp.

AD #1   YOUR QUALIFICATIONS

AD #2

Part 5

ANSWERING AN AD

Objective: To answer a want ad

EXERCISE 1 · DIFFERENT WAYS TO ANSWER AN AD

There are different ways to answer a want ad: by telephoning, by writing or by going in person.

Look at the following want ads. How would you answer them?

FOR EXAMPLE:

DANCER—over 18—Exc. pay, apply in person— Larry's Lounge, 19 West 46th St.	By *going in person*

1.
ACCOUNTANT—min. 2 yrs. exp., exc. salary & benefits, send resume[1] to New York News, Box 29250	By _____

2.
FILE CLERK 8:30–12:00. Applicant must want permanent job. 891-5030	By _____

---

[1] resume: a list of your education, experience and skills (usually required for professional jobs)

3.

MECHANIC
Min. 3 yrs. exp. Send resume to Arctic Co. 699 College Ave., Boston, Mass.

By _____

4.

RECEPTIONIST
Job requires typing, general office experience. Minimum typing speed 60 W.P.M. Electric typewriter. Write this paper Box No. 3541.

By _____

5.

RESTAURANT   HELP.
Waiters, Waitresses, Bartenders. Exper. only. Nicky's Restaurant, 642 Broadway. Apply Wed.– Fri. 2–4 P.M.

By _____

6.

SECRETARIES   General
secretarial duties h.s. grad. 50 wpm. 1 yr exp. Cathy McNabb 792-4990

By _____

7.

SECURITY GUARDS
Full & part-time openings immediately for guards. Must present a good appearance. Good salary & benefits, own car & phone. Apply Mon. 12 Noon to 5 P.M., Tues. & Wed. 9 A.M. to 4 P.M. Granada Inn and ask for Mr. Linsner or call 342-7741 for appointment.

By _____

8.

TELLERS
Experienced bank tellers, 9–12 months experience required. City Bank, 500 5th Ave. Apply 10–12:30 Personnel [1] EOE

By _____

9.

TYPIST
10-key adding machine. Apply in person, Bay Lumber Co. 801 Dumont St.

By _____

10.

WAITERS AND WAIT-
RESSES Experience required. Closed Sundays and holidays. Salary + benefits—Average $200 weekly. 821-1330

By _____

[1] Personnel: the department that hires the employees of a company

EXERCISE 2 · WRITING TO A NEWSPAPER

A. To answer some ads, you have to write to the newspaper.

Look at the want ad index of the *San Francisco Times*. Circle the address of the paper.

```
┌─────────────────────────────────────────────────────────────────────┐
│                        WANT AD INDEX                                  │
│                                                                       │
│   CATEGORY NUMBERS      RATES: (2 line min.)                          │
│                                                                       │
│   Auto Sales      580   Personals                TO ANSWER A TIMES    │
│   Business        149     1–30 times—$4.50 a line  NUMBER AD          │
│   Help Wanted     147   Commercial                                    │
│   Jobs Wanted     124     1–2 times—$4.00 a line Address mail to:     │
│   Merchandise     550     3–5 times—$3.65 a line Ad No.               │
│   Personals       213     6–13 times—$3.15 a line San Francisco Times │
│   Real Estate     378     14–30 times—$2.75 a line 325 Mission St.    │
│   Rentals         300                            San Francisco, CA 92203 │
│   Services        101   Call 741-2000 to place ads                    │
└─────────────────────────────────────────────────────────────────────┘
```

Some ads give an ad number or box number to write to.

Look at the ad below. Circle the ad number.

```
┌─────────────────────────┐
│ CLERK-TYPIST—            │
│ bilingual, English       │
│ and Spanish. 1 yr.       │
│ exp. Export com-         │
│ pany. Write this         │
│ paper Ad No. 29325       │
└─────────────────────────┘
```

To address an envelope, use the ad number or box number, the name of the company and the address.

Look at the example below.

```
Eduardo Rodriguez
35 Capp Street
San Francisco, CA 94110



                        Ad No. 29325
                        San Francisco Times
                        325 Mission Street
                        San Francisco, CA 92203
```

Now find an ad in your local newspaper that gives an ad number or a box number. Address this envelope to answer the ad.

B. Read the want ad.

> **SALES CLERK.** P/T or F/T for ladies clothing factory. Previous sales work helpful. Must do physical work. Write to *S.F. Times* Ad #3952

When you write a letter to answer an ad, give the job title, the name of the paper, your qualifications and how the employer can contact you.

Clara Moran answered the ad. Read her letter. Then answer the questions on page 45.

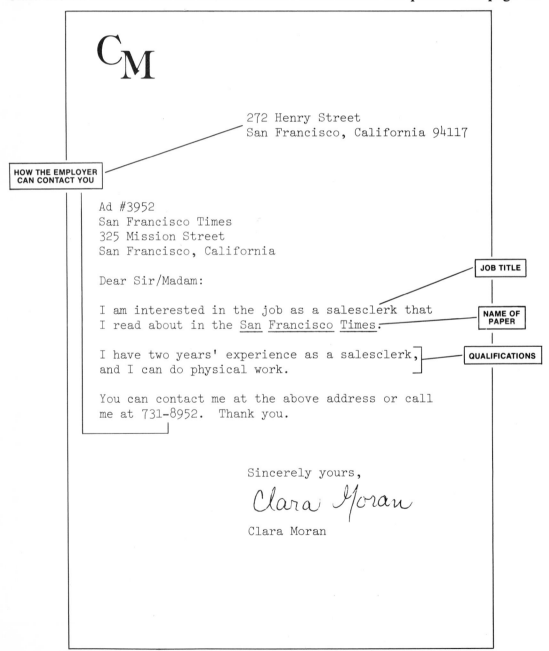

C~M~

272 Henry Street
San Francisco, California 94117

HOW THE EMPLOYER
CAN CONTACT YOU

Ad #3952
San Francisco Times
325 Mission Street
San Francisco, California

Dear Sir/Madam:

I am interested in the job as a salesclerk that
I read about in the San Francisco Times.

JOB TITLE

NAME OF PAPER

I have two years' experience as a salesclerk,
and I can do physical work.

QUALIFICATIONS

You can contact me at the above address or call
me at 731-8952. Thank you.

Sincerely yours,

Clara Moran

Clara Moran

1. What job is Clara interested in?

2. Where did she read about it?

3. What experience does she have?

4. What else can she do?

5. Where can the employer contact her?

EXERCISE 3 · THE INFORMATION YOU NEED

After you decide which ads to answer, it is a good idea to write down the information that you will need to apply for the job.

FOR EXAMPLE:

> **HOTEL HELP WANTED**
> Front Desk Clerk for 100-room hotel. 1 year experience, Good salary and benefits, health insurance. Apply in person: Manager's office, King's Way Inn, 420 Holladay St., Trenton, New Jersey

INFORMATION TO USE

1. JOB TITLE _Front desk clerk_

2. WHERE TO GO OR WRITE _Kings Way Inn_
   420 Holladay St., Trenton
   WHAT NUMBER TO CALL _____

3. WHO TO ASK FOR _Manager_

4. WHEN TO APPLY _____

5. HECTOR RIVERA'S QUALIFICATIONS _2 yrs. exp._

Choose two want ads from your local newspaper. Write down the information that you would need to apply for each job.

AD #1

INFORMATION TO USE

1. JOB TITLE _____

2. WHERE TO GO OR WRITE _____

   _____

   WHAT NUMBER TO CALL _____

3. WHO TO ASK FOR _____

4. WHEN TO APPLY _____

5. YOUR QUALIFICATIONS _____

AD #2

INFORMATION TO USE

1. JOB TITLE _____

2. WHERE TO GO OR WRITE _____

   _____

   WHAT NUMBER TO CALL _____

3. WHO TO ASK FOR _____

4. WHEN TO APPLY _____

5. YOUR QUALIFICATIONS _____

One way to answer an ad is by telephoning. In this unit you will hear several applicants call about jobs. You will learn how to introduce yourself to an interviewer from the examples. A good introduction will help you get an appointment for an interview.

Will They Call You?

Part 1

BEGINNING THE CALL

Objective: To get the right person or the right department on the telephone

EXERCISE 1 · WHO TO ASK FOR

The first step in calling about a job is to ask for a person, a department or an extension number. Some ads only give a telephone number. Other ads give the name of a person, the personnel department or an extension number.

You will hear several conversations that show some different ways to begin a call about a job. First, read the ads and decide what you would say to begin the call. Then listen to the calls. What does each caller say?

> **FILE CLERK/TYPIST**
> Busy sales office, gd. co. benefits. Call Joan at 574-8860. An equal oppty. employer

CALL #1 _____

> **AUTO PAINTER WANTED**
> Small shop in St. Louis. Exc. sal. for right person. 692-3024. Ask for Mr. Baker.

CALL #2 _____

> **RECEPTIONIST/PHONE OPERATOR**, lite typing 981-2760 ext. 19

CALL #3 _____

> **NURSES** Aide needed for small medical group in Philadelphia. F/T. Exp. pref. Call 583-4220 ext. 31

CALL #4 _____

> **INSURANCE TYPIST—**
> Must be good, accurate typist. Prev. ofc. exp. desired. Equal Opportunity Employer. PERSONNEL 981-7600

CALL #5 _____

> **SALESPERSON—**F/T
> perm. employment, vac. & holidays. Appliance Parts Company 494-7700

CALL #6 _____

EXERCISE 2 · WHAT TO SAY

Listen to some different ways to begin a call about a job, and fill in the blanks.

1. *When the ad gives the name of a person:*

SALESPERSON exp. for record company. Call Barbara 433-1092 8–4.

NOTE
May and could have the same meaning in these sentences. You can also use can. May and could are more polite than can.

a. _____ I speak _____ Barbara, please?

TYPIST Part time 2 or 3 days week. 421-8485 Ms. Jones.

b. May _____ _____ _____ Ms. Jones, please?

2. *When the ad gives an extension number:*

a. _____ I _____ extension 31, _____?
b. _____ 31, please.

TELEPHONE Operators needed. Transportation nec. Phone 468-3700 Ext. 31

3. *When the ad gives only a telephone number or says, "Personnel Department":*

NURSES AIDES Certified. St. Francis Hospital 755-9515

a. _____ I have _____ personnel department, _____?

MEDICAL Secty. Bilingual Cantonese & Eng. Perm. P/T 838-9722 Personnel Dept.

b. _____ department, please.

EXERCISE 3 · BEGINNING YOUR CALL

Role-Play: Receptionist and Applicant

Read the want ads. Decide what you would say to begin the call. Then choose a partner, and practice beginning your call.

FOR EXAMPLE:

> **CLERK TYPIST** Must be able to type 60 wpm. Answer phone & general office duties. Call Roger Braden 697-5510 for appt.
> HIGHLAND CORPORATION
> Equal Opportunity Employer

Receptionist: Good afternoon. Highland Corporation.

Applicant: *May I speak to Mr. Braden, please?*

Receptionist: Just one moment, please.

1.
> **PAINTER**
> Exper. painting. Soon as possible. 668-4194 Ext. 21

Receptionist: 668-4194

Applicant: _____

Receptionist: Thank you.

2.
FILE CLERK for Spears Co.—Call 982-7036 Personnel

Receptionist: Good morning. Spears Company.

Applicant: _____

Receptionist: Mr. Evans is on another line [1] right now. Could you hold [2] for a minute?

Applicant: _____

3.
SECRETARY. Exp. required, good phone voice. Ask for Mr. Nelson, 873-1797.

Receptionist: Nelson's Sporting Goods. May I help you?

Applicant: _____

Receptionist: Oh, no, he's not in [3] right now. Could you call back in about ten minutes?

Applicant: _____

4.
COMPUTER OPERATOR. Min. 1 yr. exp. Gd. oppty. Call 434-0377.

Receptionist: Good afternoon. American Electronics.

Applicant: _____

Receptionist: One moment, please.

Applicant: _____

5.
RECEPTIONIST/Phone Operator, Lite typing. 981-2760 Ext. 62. ELKIN TRAVEL

Receptionist: _____

Applicant: _____

Receptionist: _____

Applicant: _____

---

[1] on another line: talking to someone on another telephone line

[2] hold: wait

[3] in: in the office

Part 2

TALKING TO THE RECEPTIONIST

Objective: To answer the receptionist's questions

EXERCISE 1 · WHAT A RECEPTIONIST MIGHT ASK

When you call about a job, the receptionist might ask what your name is or what you are calling about. This often happens when a company does not have a personnel department. This can also happen when the receptionist is responsible for getting information about callers. Sometimes the receptionist needs to find out where the call should go or how important the call is.

1. **Read the first want ad.**

> **WAREHOUSE ASST.**
> Mon– Fri. 9–5 647-5243.

Now listen to a call about the ad. Listen carefully to what the receptionist says. Then answer the questions.

a. What does the receptionist say?

b. What is the caller's answer?

2. **Read the second want ad.**

> **CLERK TYPIST,** Gen. ofc.
> Phones, Exp. pref. 981-
> 6212 Personnel.

Now listen to the call. Listen carefully to what the receptionist asks. Then answer the questions.

a. What does the receptionist ask the caller?

b. Why does she ask for this information?

EXERCISE 2 · WHAT YOU ARE CALLING ABOUT

There are different ways to say what you are calling about. A common way is:

> **PRINTER** [1]—New co. needs qual. person. Call 621-1440.

"I'm calling about the job as a printer."

Practice saying what you are calling about. Use the job titles below or other jobs you would like to apply for.

1. **CLERK-TYPIST**—1 yr. exp. req. Call Carol 764-3850.

6. **RECEPTIONIST.** Good typing, exp. helpful. Call 490-2000 for appt.

2. **AUTO MECHANIC** Harry's Garage, 591-2664.

7.

3. **BANK TELLER**—National Bank, Personnel, 678-3425.

8.

4. **WELDER.** Call Mike 359-8271.

9.

5. **MACHINE OPERATOR** Must have prev. exp. Call 963-4962.

10.

---

[1] printer: a person who uses a machine to make copies of books and other printed material

EXERCISE 3 · ANSWERING THE RECEPTIONIST'S QUESTIONS

Role-Play: Receptionist and Applicant

Read the ads. Decide what you would say to the receptionist. Then choose a partner, and practice what you would say.

FOR EXAMPLE:

> **FILE CLERK.** Alphabetical filing, previous exper. not req. Exc. salary & benefits. Mrs. Mitchell 392-2064 EOE M/F

Receptionist: Good morning. Farmer's Insurance.

Applicant: *May I speak to Mrs. Mitchell, please?*

Receptionist: Yes. Who's calling, please?

Applicant: *This is (your name).*

> NOTE
> There are different ways for receptionists to ask for your name. They might ask:
>
> "What is your name, please?"
> "May I ask who's calling, please?"
> "May I tell him/her who's calling, please?"
> "Could you give me your name, please?"
> "Could I have your name, please?"

1.

| ACCOUNTING CLERK |
| Exp. helpful. Room to ad-
vance. Good sal. Call
364-7000 |

Receptionist: Portman Company.

Applicant: _____

Receptionist: What are you calling about, please?

Applicant: _____

> **NOTE**
> There are different ways
> for receptionists to ask
> what you are calling
> about. They might ask:
>
> "What are you inquiring
>   about?"
> "What is this in reference
>   to?"
> "May I ask what you're
>   calling about?"

2.

| CARPENTER—w/gen.
bldg. skills. Must have
own tools and trans.
771-2433 ext. 18 |

Receptionist: Good afternoon. Complete Builders.

Applicant: _____

Receptionist: Thank you. Could I have your name, please?

Applicant: _____

3.

| ELECTRICIAN—Entry
level w/some electronics
exp. Please call or write
to Electronic Retail Sys-
tems, 221 Columbus Ave.,
New York, New York
10023 (212) 595-7900 |

Receptionist: 7900.

Applicant: _____

Receptionist: We don't have a personnel department.
What is this in reference to?

Applicant: _____

EXERCISE 4 · IF THERE IS NO PERSONNEL DEPARTMENT

Sometimes you will know from the want ad that the company does not have a personnel department. For example, small companies, small stores, doctors' offices or private employment agencies [1] do not have personnel departments. Tell the receptionist what you are calling about when there is no personnel department. (If you are not sure, ask for the personnel department.)

Look at the want ads below. Put a check next to the ads of employers that probably do not have personnel departments.

BANK TELLER
Part Time. Experience preferred. Apply Bank of Colorado. 1000 Taraval, Denver 661-7070. Equal opportunity employer. m/f.

DENTAL ASST. P/T Tues., Wed. & Fri. Only exp. person should apply. 756-4388

ELECTRONICS CAREER OPPORTUNITIES
M/F Applicants must have 2 years' exp. Company benefits include excellent Medical and Dental plans. Please apply Mon. through Wed. 8:30 A.M.–1 P.M.
370 THIRD ST.
TELEPHONE NATIONAL

SERVICE STATION attendant, exp. $3 hour. 863-8115

HAIR STYLIST good working cond. in new shop. 368-1114.

HOTEL SECRETARY—
Typing 50–60 wpm, good phone voice. Busy office 421-1000

DAVIDS AGENCY 870 Mkt. 362-3120 Chef. Driver. Cook.

NEWSPAPER
Telephone public relations. Permanent, part-time job. Must be dependable, organized. CALL 221-0272 NEW YORK NEWS.

CLERICAL WORKERS—
good phone and typing skills needed. Gen. ofc. responsibilities. BRADY AGENCY—223-8660 100% Free

SECRETARY—Doctor's office Min. 2 yrs. exper. Spanish speaking. 788-7300

NOTE
Sometimes agencies list several job titles. Tell the receptionist which job you are calling about.

---

[1] employment agencies: companies that help people find jobs

Part 3
INTRODUCING YOURSELF

Objective: To introduce yourself to an interviewer

EXERCISE 1 · THREE THINGS TO SAY

After you talk to the receptionist, you will usually talk to an interviewer. You should introduce yourself to this person. Tell him or her your name, what job you are calling about and how you found out about the job.

Listen to these calls. Then answer the questions for each call.

CALL #1   a. What is the caller's name?

b. What is she calling about?

c. How did she find out about it?

CALL #2   a. What is he calling about?

b. How did he find out about the job?

c. Did he introduce himself well?

CALL #3   a. What is he calling about?

b. How did he find out about the job?

c. Did he introduce himself well?

EXERCISE 2 · HOW YOU FOUND OUT

A.

There are different ways to say how you found out about a job. If you found out about it in the want ads, you can say, "I read about it in (*the name of the paper*)."

If you found out about it from a person or an agency, you can say, "I was referred by (*the name of the person or agency*)." If the person is unknown to the company, you should say, "I was referred by a friend."

Now practice saying how you found out about a job. Use the information below.

FOR EXAMPLE: the *New York Times*   "I read about it in the *New York Times*."

or

a friend   "I was referred by *a friend.*"

1. the *Miami Sun*
2. a friend
3. the State Employment Agency
4. the *Chicago Tribune*
5. Mr. Robert Thompson
6. the American Personnel Service
7. the *San Francisco Examiner*
8. Mr. Hines, the accountant of the company

B.

Now practice introducing yourself to a partner. Use the information below.

FOR EXAMPLE: (name), nurse's aide, the *Detroit News*

"My name is _____. I'm calling about the job as a nurse's aide. I read about it in the *Detroit News*."

1. (name), file clerk, the *Los Angeles Times*
2. (name), electrician, Mr. Charles Smith
3. (name), bookkeeper, the State Employment Agency
4. (name), general office clerk, the *Boston Globe*
5. (name), printer, a friend
6. (*name*), *a job you would like to apply for, your local newspaper*

EXERCISE 3 · A REVIEW OF WHAT TO SAY

Here are some applicants who are introducing themselves to the interviewer over the phone. Fill in the blanks with the words they should use.

1. My name _____ Barbara Wilson. I'm calling about the

   _____ as a general office clerk. I read _____ it in the

   Detroit News.

2. _____ _____ is David Gomez. I'm

   _____ about the job _____ a welder. I read about it

   _____ the *Times.*

3. This _____ Lucy Tam. _____ calling about the job as

   _____ bookkeeper. I _____ referred by Mr. Frank

   Sheldon.

4. _____ is Steven White. I'm _____

   _____ the job _____ _____ repairman.

   I was referred _____ the Morrison Employment Agency.

EXERCISE 4 · MAKING YOUR INTRODUCTION

Role-Play: Interviewer and Applicant

Read the job announcements. Decide what you would say to the interviewer over the phone. Then choose a partner, and practice introducing yourself.

FOR EXAMPLE:
An ad in the
Atlanta Constitution

WAREHOUSE ASSIS-
TANT, High School grad.
Must know mech. & elec-
tronics $3.50 per hour +
benefits. American Tele-
phone Supplies. 692-3295

Interviewer: Yes, may I help you?

Applicant: *My name is ——. I'm calling about the job as a warehouse assistant. I read about it in the Atlanta Constitution.*

1. An ad in your local newspaper

BOOKKEEPER/ Secretar-
ial. Part time, flexible hrs.
exp. req. 731-0445. Call
Sue.

Interviewer: Hello. Sue Morris.

Applicant: _____

_____

2. Referred by Jobs Incorporated

SALESPERSON. Part time
mornings. Sales exper.
helpful. Call 647–7926

Interviewer: Personnel. Mr. Rosenberg speaking.

Applicant: _____

_____

3. Referred by the State Employment Agency

MACHINIST. General exp. pref.
Should have training.
Medical, dental & insurance.
Los Angeles (213) 445–6790

Interviewer: Sam Rogers.

Applicant: _____

_____

4. A friend tells you about a job as a keypunch operator at the telephone company.

Interviewer: Personnel department. Miss Cooper.

Applicant: _____

_____

Part 4

GIVING YOUR QUALIFICATIONS

Objective: To give your qualifications for a specific job

EXERCISE 1 · AFTER THE INTRODUCTION

After you introduce yourself to the interviewer, you should be ready to give your qualifications for the job. Talk about your experience, education and skills that relate to the requirements of the job. Interviewers want to know if you are qualified before they see you.

1. Read the first want ad.

> **CLERK TYPIST**—must be good, accurate typist. Prev. ofc. exp. desired. Call Marsha. 664-6630.

Now listen to a call about the job. Listen for the information that the applicant gives. Then answer the questions.

a. How did the caller find out about the job?

b. How fast does he type?

c. How much office experience does he have?

d. What information in the ad helped him give his qualifications?

2. Read the second want ad.

> **MECHANIC,** motorcycles. min. 2 yrs. exp. w/Hondas—gd. oppty. & benefits. EOE M/F D&D Cycles, 355-7111 ext. 31.

If the interviewer does not ask you about your qualifications, it is a good idea to offer this information.

Listen to this call, and answer the questions.

a. What information does the caller give when he introduces himself?

b. Does he have the requirements for the job?

c. What are his other qualifications?

EXERCISE 2 · DIFFERENT WAYS TO GIVE YOUR QUALIFICATIONS

A. There are several different ways to give your qualifications.

Read the examples. Then practice what an applicant might say for each job.

EXAMPLES:

| RECEPTIONIST — 1 yr. exp. full time. Call Bill 821-3280. |

I have 1 year's experience as a receptionist.

NOTE
Always give the number of years' (or months') experience you have.

| WELDER—min. 2 yrs. exp. req. Good benefits 789-4200. |

I have 3 years' experience as a welder.

1. | CASHIER—1 yr. exp. 8–5 P.M. daily. Good. sal. 821-3000 | _____

2. | MECHANIC—5 yrs. exp. Call A.M. 331-6000 ext. 12 | _____

3. | TYPIST—min. 2 yrs. exp. 65 wpm. Write this paper Ad 3160 | _____

4. | APARTMENT MANAGER 1 yr. exp. pref. 165 Brown St., Omaha. | _____

5. | BOOKKEEPER—Some exp. pref. Call 381-6201 | _____

6. *A job that you would like to apply for; the number of years' experience you have*

_____

_____

B. Read the examples. Then practice what an applicant might say for each kind of work.

EXAMPLES:

GEN. OFC. CLERK, 2 yrs. ofc. exp. Call 663-1077	*I have 2 years' office experience.*
CARPENTER—F/T, prev. building exp. helpful. Write this paper—ad 1628	*I have 3 years' building experience.*

1. **SECRETARY FOR LARGE OFFICE** 2 yrs. clerical exp. Call 651-3181—Sue

2. **CLERK-TYPIST** prev. ofc. exp. typ. 70 wpm. Accurate. Personnel 822-3341 ext. 20

3. **RECEPTIONIST** — Part time 1 yr. typing exp. pref. call Mary 221-6000

4. **SALESMAN** — TV-Stereo co. some electronics exp. req. Apply in person— Atlantic Stereo. 2101 Brush St., Cincinnati.

5. **NURSE'S AIDE**—hospital exp. helpful—must work nights—call 821-1000

6. *The number of years' experience you have for the job you would like to apply for*

C. Read the example. Then practice what an applicant might say for each skill.

EXAMPLE:

> **MAINTENANCE MECHANIC**—1 yr. exp. repair equipment, use elec. tools, apply in person. 1020 Second Ave. NYC

I can repair equipment.

1.

> **MECHANIC**
> Repair cars, help with trucks. Jim's GARAGE — Corner 1st & Spruce St. Detroit.

_____

2.

> **ASST. ACCOUNTANT** F/T Type 50 wpm. some exp. req. AD# 12110

_____

3.

> **CARPENTER HELPER.**
> Build cabinets, no exp. req. 821-6200

_____

4.

> **CHEF**—Full time, plan menu, cook Italian food 543-9036 eves.

_____

5.

> **GENERAL CLERK**—P/T answer phones, typ. req. Call 527-8047

_____

D. Read the example. Then practice what an applicant might say for each skill.

EXAMPLE:

| INSURANCE SECTY. Filing, must typ. 70 wpm.—Call 647-7927 | *I can do filing, and I can type 75 words a minute.* |

1.

| MAINTENANCE MECHANIC Equip. repair, <u>maintenance work.</u> 311-8111 ext. 42 | |

2.

| ASST. MANAGER—<u>sales work,</u> oppty. to advance in company. 626-1443 | |

3.

| MACHINIST. exp. req., <u>welding.</u> Industrial Service Co. 2700 C St., Sacramento | |

4.

| BANK CLERK—Person with gd. <u>bookkeeping.</u> Apply Golden Bank—300 Maine, Milwaukee | |

5.

| CONSTRUCTION—Exp. pref. <u>carpentry,</u> some electrical work 221-1000 | |

6. *A skill that you have*

E. Read the example. Then practice what an applicant might say for each piece of equipment.

EXAMPLE:

> **GEN. OFC. CLERK**—M/F typing, filing, 10-key adding machine. Call 331-9800—personnel.

I can use a 10-Key adding machine.

1. > **BOOKKEEPER**—full or P/T, use of calculator,[1] lite typ./filing. Resume this paper Ad 10056

2. > **RECEPTIONIST,** typing, filing, dictaphone.[2] Gd. sal. & ben. apply in person. 120 3rd St.

3. > **MAINTENANCE PERSON** — use of floor polisher,[3] 1 yr. exp. must work nights. Call Meg 881-0112

4. > **MECHANIC**—M/F—must be able to use lathe.[4] Work 2 shifts. Apply in person 253 S. Main.

5. *Equipment or tools that you can use* _____

_____

_____

---

[1] calculator: an electronic machine that adds, subtracts, multiplies and divides

[2] dictaphone: a machine used to record information that will be typed

[3] floor polisher: a machine that shines floors

[4] lathe: a machine that changes the shape of metal by turning it against a tool

F. Read the examples. Then practice what an applicant might say for each requirement.

EXAMPLES:

ACCT.—F/T, ten-key add. mach. Must be gd. w/fig. Call 668-1001	*I'm good with figures.*
CARPENTER—gen. bldg. skills. Must have own transp. Write this paper AD 2702	*I have my own car.*

1. | **DANCERS,** must be over 21. Elegant Nightclub. Apply in person DINO'S LOUNGE 268 O'Farrell | _____

2. | **ELECTRICIAN.** Must have insurance 664-6500 | _____

3. | **SECTY**—dwntwn ofc., must be bilingual— French & English. Call 331-1011 | _____

4. | **CASHIER**—some bkkpg. exp. must be h.s. grad. call A.M. only 771-8012 EOE | _____

5. | **MECHANIC**—no exp. req. must have own tools. Call Frank—527-8017 | _____

G. Sometimes you have studied something in school that makes you qualified for a job.
Read the examples. Then practice what an applicant might say for each field of work.

EXAMPLES:

| ELECTRICIAN—no exp. req., but must know electronics. Will train, call Bob—346-2020 | *I studied electronics in school.* |

| GEN. CLERK—typing, filing req., bookkeeping pref. call 848-3442 ext. 12 | *I studied bookkeeping in school.* |

1. GAS STATION ATTENDANT—Full time. Must know auto mechanics. Apply at Olympic Station—18th & Sands.

2. ASST. BOOKKEEPER—lite typing. Must know some accounting, call 881-7700 EOE

3. MECHANIC—repairs on all types of electrical systems. Welding req. write this paper—Box No. 2301

4. OFFICE MANAGER—Insurance co. Must know keypunch. Call Sandra in Personnel 653-1581

5. GEN. OFFICE—typing, good w/figures. Shorthand req. call Billie 861-1111 EOE M/F

H. Sometimes you do not have all the qualifications, but you still want to apply for the job. You should be positive when you talk about a qualification that you do not have.

Read the examples. Then practice what you would say if you did not have the qualifications below.

EXAMPLES:

SECRETARY—type 60 wpm., file, <u>use dictaphone</u>, good oppty. to advance. 852-9178	*I've never used a dictaphone, but I'd like to learn.*
ACCOUNTING CLERK—type 40 wpm, 10-key adding mach. Some exp. <u>pref.</u> Personnel 543-9036	*I don't have experience as an accounting clerk, but I learn quickly.*

1. CLERK TYPIST—gd. typing and ability to work w/fig. <u>Some ofc. exp.</u> Boston Agency, Inc. 112 Boylston.

2. BOOKKEEPER Lt. typing, <u>use 10-key and calculator.</u> Dwntwn. ofc. call St. Clair's 282-4900

3. MAINTENANCE—<u>plumbing exp. pref.</u> Must have own car & tools. 648-5220

4. MACHINIST—2 yrs. exp., <u>use lathe</u> & drill. Good oppty. & ben. Call Ben 583-0164

5. *A qualification that you do not have for the job you want*

EXERCISE 3 · A REVIEW OF THE WORDS TO USE

⬛••

Read the ads. Then listen to the applicants' qualifications for the jobs. Fill in the blanks.

1. | **RECEPTIONIST**—Typ. 60 wpm, dictaphone, filing. Geology Satellite Co. $750/mo. 981-6265 |

    "I _____ type 60 words a minute. I can
    _____ a dictaphone, and I can
    _____ filing."

2. | **MAINTENANCE** Person w/prev. carpentry exp. must use elec. tools and build cabinets. Write to P.O. Box 1788, San Mateo 94402 |

    "I _____ four years' carpentry experience,
    and I can _____ electrical tools. I've
    _____ built cabinets, but I learn
    _____."

3. | **BOOKKEEPER**—1 yr. exp. req. must know some accntg, and be gd w/fig. Contact John Miller. Ext. 439, 632-9421 EOE M/F |

    "I have one year's experience _____
    _____ bookkeeper. I _____
    accounting in school, and I'm good _____
    figures."

4. | **AUTO MECHANIC**—min. 2 yrs. exp. must know some welding and have own tools. Afternoon shift, apply in person, 2778 Cobb Rd. |

    "I have three _____ experience as
    _____ auto mechanic. I _____
    welding _____ school, and I have
    _____ _____ tools."

5. | **CASHIER**—full time, gd. salary & benefits. H.S. grad. Lite typing, cashier exp. pref. 621-4200 |

    "I _____ _____ high school
    graduate, and I can _____ light
    _____. I don't have _____ as a
    cashier, but _____ like to learn."

EXERCISE 4 · YOUR QUALIFICATIONS

Practice giving your qualifications. Write as many sentences as you can.

"I CAN...."

"I HAVE...."

"I CAN DO...."

"I CAN USE...."

"I AM...."

"I STUDIED"....

"I'VE NEVER...."

1. _____

_____

2. _____

_____

3. _____

_____

4. _____

_____

5. _____

_____

6. _____

_____

7. _____

_____

EXERCISE 5 · WHAT YOU WOULD SAY

When you learned how to use the want ads, you listed your qualifications for two jobs. Now you should be ready to give your qualifications to the interviewer.

Use the ads that you chose before (page 39), or choose two new ads from your local newspaper. First, list your qualifications. Then write what you would say to the interviewer.

FOR EXAMPLE:

BANK TELLER—Exp. req., typ. 40 wpm. Full time. Good benefits. Call 764-3970 Personnel. EOE

JULIA FANO'S QUALIFICATIONS

WHAT SHE WOULD SAY

teller - 6 mos. exp.   *I have six months' experience as a teller.*

type 40 wpm   *I can type 40 words a minute.*

1 yr. gen. ofc. work exp.   *I have one year's general office work experience.*

YOUR QUALIFICATIONS

WHAT YOU WOULD SAY

AD #1 _____

AD #2 _____

Part 5
MAKING THE APPOINTMENT

Objective: To get the information you need for the appointment

EXERCISE 1 · THE INFORMATION YOU NEED TO GET

A. Listen to the end of a call about a job. The caller is making an appointment for an interview. Listen for the information that he receives. Then answer the questions.

1. What time is Steve's interview?

2. What is the date of the interview?

3. What is the address?

4. What are the cross streets?

5. Who should he ask for?

B. Listen to the end of another call. Listen for the information that the caller receives. Then answer the questions.

1. What is the time and date of the interview?

2. What is the address?

3. Who should he ask for?

4. Does the applicant get all the information?

5. Does he have enough time to write down the information?

6. Why does he repeat all the information?

EXERCISE 2 · WRITING DOWN THE INFORMATION

When you make an appointment for an interview, always repeat the information slowly. This will help you confirm [1] the information and give you enough time to write it down.

Listen to the following conversations. Write down the information as the caller repeats it.

FOR EXAMPLE:

You write: *4 p.m. Monday, May 8.*

1. _____

2. _____

3. _____

4. _____

5. _____

6. _____

7. _____

8. _____

9. _____

10. _____

[1] confirm: repeat information to be sure it is correct

[2] How about: one way to offer a time for an appointment
         Some other ways are:
         What about _____ ?
         Could you come in at _____ ?
         Is _____ OK?
         Is _____ convenient?

[3] That's: used to repeat information

EXERCISE 3 · ASKING FOR THE INFORMATION

When you make an appointment, you might need to ask these questions:

> "What's the address?"
> "What are the cross streets?"
> "Who should I ask for?"
> "How do you spell your last name?"

Can you ask questions for these answers?

FOR EXAMPLE: **Applicant:** _What's the address?_

Interviewer: "175 Church Street."

1. **Applicant:** _____

   Interviewer: "It's between Second and Third Avenue."

2. **Applicant:** _____

   Interviewer: "Ask for Ruth Silver."

3. **Applicant:** _____

   Interviewer: "S-I-L-V-E-R."

4. **Applicant:** _____

   Interviewer: "32 Linn Street."

5. **Applicant:** _____

   Interviewer: "It's between Castro and Diamond Boulevard."

6. **Applicant:** _____

   Interviewer: "Ask for Mr. Dixson."

7. **Applicant:** _____

   Interviewer: "That's D-I-X-S-O-N."

8. **Applicant:** _____

   Interviewer: "The address is 120 Brooks Road."

EXERCISE 4 · NUMBERS IN STREET ADDRESSES

You say numbers differently when they are in street addresses.

Read the examples. Then practice saying the addresses.

A. EXAMPLES: 37 Main St.—"Thirty-seven Main Street."
              237 Main St.—"Two-thirty-seven Main Street."
           1037 Main St.—"Ten-thirty-seven Main Street."
           2137 Main St.—"Twenty-one-thirty-seven Main Street."
       21379 Main St.—"Two-one-three-seven-nine Main Street."

1. 47 State Blvd.
2. 527 Miller Ave.
3. 1082 Green Rd.
4. 32163 Market St.
5. 1120 Baker Ave.

B. EXAMPLES: 200 Main St.—"Two hundred Main Street."
           1000 Main St.—"One thousand Main Street."
           1100 Main St.—"Eleven hundred Main Street."

1. 300 Michigan Ave.
2. 2000 White Rd.
3. 1200 Ocean Ave.
4. 4000 Third St.
5. 4100 Adams Rd.

C. EXAMPLES: 201 Main St.—"Two-oh-one Main Street."
           1001 Main St.—"One-oh-oh-one Main Street."
           1101 Main St.—"Eleven-oh-one Main Street."

> **NOTE**
> 1001 is sometimes said "One thousand one."

1. 501 Second St.
2. 2001 Washington St.
3. 1201 Fourth Ave.
4. 5002 River Rd.
5. 5102 Lake St.

D. Review
1. 400 State St.
2. 404 Ocean Ave.
3. 434 River Rd.
4. 6005 Market St.
5. 6145 Michigan Ave.
6. 10735 Maple Blvd.

EXERCISE 5 · GETTING THE INFORMATION

Practice making an appointment for an interview. Look at the questions and answers in the example. Notice that the applicant confirms the information and writes it down.

EXAMPLE:

INTERVIEWER	APPLICANT
Date and time "How about Tuesday, October 4th at 1 P.M.?"	"That's Tuesday, October 4th at 1 P.M. What's the address?"
Address "The address is 47 Michigan Avenue."	"That's 47 Michigan Avenue. What are the cross streets?"
Cross streets "It's between Washington and Adams Road."	"That's between Washington and Adams Road. Who should I ask for?"
Name "Ask for Jerry Walton."	"That's Jerry Walton. How do you spell the last name?"
Spelling "W-A-L-T-O-N."	"That's W-A-L-T-O-N."

APPLICANT'S NOTES

Date and time	*Tues., Oct. 4, 1 P.M.*
Address	*47 Michigan Avenue*
Cross streets	*Washington + Adams Rd.*
Name	*Jerry Walton*

Now choose a partner, and practice making an appointment for an interview. The interviewer will give the information below. The applicant will take notes on page 79.

INTERVIEWER

> **GUIDE**
> "How about . . . ?"
> "The address is . . . ."
> "It's between . . . ."
> "Ask for . . . ."

CALL #1

Date and time	Monday, June 3, 10:30 A.M.
Address	301 Green Road
Cross streets	Second and Third Street
Name	Chris Turner

CALL #2

Date and time	Thursday, February 2, 9:00 A.M.
Address	3815 Fourth Avenue
Cross streets	Miller and Baker Street
Name	Linda Cortina

CALL #3

Date and time	Tomorrow, 3:30 P.M.
Address	534 Fourth Avenue
Cross streets	Market and Ocean Avenue
Name	Pat Murphy

APPLICANT'S NOTES

```
GUIDE
"What's the address?"
"What are the cross streets?"
"Who should I ask for?"
"How do you spell the last name?"
```

CALL #1

Date and time
Address
Cross streets
Name

CALL #2

Date and time
Address
Cross streets
Name

CALL #3

Date and time
Address
Cross streets
Name

EXERCISE 6 · A REAL CALL

Choose an ad with a telephone number from your local newspaper. Use the worksheet below to plan your call.

INFORMATION TO USE

Job title
What number to call
Who to ask for
When to apply
Your qualifications

Now use that information to call about the job. Try to get an appointment for an interview. Write down all the information you get from the interviewer on the worksheet below.

INFORMATION TO GET

Appointment date & time
Address
Cross streets
Interviewer's name

UNIT
FIVE

What's Their Opinion?

In this unit you will hear interviewers talk about certain things they look for in job applicants. As you listen to their suggestions, think about how to prepare yourself for a successful interview.

Part 1
APPLICATION FORMS

Objective: To fill out an application form neatly, accurately and completely

INTRODUCTION

Before you listen to the recording, study the vocabulary below. Then discuss the Focus Questions.

VOCABULARY

1. **ability:** how well you can do something
   —Her *ability* to speak two languages helped her get the job.

2. **employment record:** list of past jobs
   —His *employment record* includes jobs as an apartment manager, a carpenter and a painter.

3. **fill out:** complete (a form)
   —An application form is usually *filled out* in ink.

4. **gap:** the time between
   —There was a long *gap* between his two jobs.

5. **handle detail:** be able to do work that requires careful attention
   —Insurance agents fill out complicated forms. They have to *handle* a lot of *detail*.

6. **impress:** make someone think well of you
   —It *impresses* the interviewer when an applicant dresses well for the interview.

7. **misspelled:** spelled wrong
   —She *misspelled* "immediately" on her application form. She only used one *m*.

Focus Questions

A. Why is it important to fill out an application form completely and accurately?

B. What names, numbers and dates do you often need on an application form?

C. Why is it important to read the directions carefully?

EXERCISE 1

Listen to the following conversations about application forms. Answer the questions after each conversation.

Conversation #1—*Harriet Miller, a personnel interviewer for a bank*

    1. What tells the interviewer about an applicant's writing ability?

    2. Before you hand in an application, what should you look for?

    3. What does Ms. Miller think of applicants who cannot handle the detail on an application form?

Conversation #2—*Marie Dumas, the personnel director for an electronics manufacturing company*

    4. What questions does Ms. Dumas ask herself when she looks at an application?

    5. What does she think when a form is incomplete?

Conversation #3—*Bill Harris, the personnel director for a large insurance company*

    6. What information about past jobs should an applicant give?

    7. What might happen to applicants who hand in incomplete application forms?

▶Does an application form tell the interviewer anything about the way you work?

EXERCISE 2

A. Look at three examples of one part of an application form. After each example, check
if it is neat, accurate and complete. Discuss your answers.

1.

APEX CORPORATION
APPLICATION FOR EMPLOYMENT

Date __5-12-80__

Position Desired __Resephionist__ Salary Desired __$650/mo.__ Referred by __Mike Garcia__

LAST NAME	FIRST	MIDDLE	SOCIAL SECURITY NO.
Anthony	Susan	B.	374-46-768

PRESENT ADDRESS	STREET	CITY	STATE	ZIP CODE	TELEPHONE NO. (503)
3642	Columbia St.	Eugene	Oregon	97488	621-4876

ARE YOU A U.S. CITIZEN

YES ☒   NO ☐

neat ☐   accurate ☐   complete ☐

2.

APEX CORPORATION
APPLICATION FOR EMPLOYMENT

Date __5-12-80__

Position Desired __Receptionist__ Salary Desired __$650/mo.__ Referred by __Mike Garcia__

LAST NAME	FIRST	MIDDLE	SOCIAL SECURITY NO.
Anthony	Susan	B.	374-846-7687

PRESENT ADDRESS	STREET	CITY	STATE	ZIP CODE	TELEPHONE NO.
3642	Columbia St.	Eugene	Oregon	97488	(503) 621-4876

ARE YOU A U.S. CITIZEN

YES ☒   NO ☒

neat ☐   accurate ☐   complete ☐

3.

APEX CORPORATION

APPLICATION FOR EMPLOYMENT

Date _____5-80_____

Position Desired _Receptionist_ Salary Desired _$650_____ Referred by _M. Garcia_

LAST NAME	FIRST	MIDDLE	SOCIAL SECURITY NO.
Anthony	Susan		374-46-7687

PRESENT ADDRESS STREET	CITY	STATE	ZIP CODE	TELEPHONE NO.
3642 Columbia	Eugene	Oregon		621-4876

ARE YOU A U.S. CITIZEN

YES ☐   NO ☐

neat ☐   **accurate** ☐   **complete** ☐

4. Now fill out the form correctly for Susan B. Anthony.

APEX CORPORATION

APPLICATION FOR EMPLOYMENT

Date _____

Position Desired _____ Salary Desired _____ Referred by _____

LAST NAME	FIRST	MIDDLE	SOCIAL SECURITY NO.

PRESENT ADDRESS STREET	CITY	STATE	ZIP CODE	TELEPHONE NO.

ARE YOU A U.S. CITIZEN

YES ☐   NO ☐

B. Now look at three examples of another part of an application form. After each example, check if it is neat, accurate and complete. Discuss your answers.

1.

SCHOOLS	NAME & LOCATION	COURSES	ATTENDED FROM MO.	YR.	TO MO.	YR.	DEGREE
HIGH OR PREP	Kennedy High Scool Portland, Oregon	ACAD. COMM. VOC. N/A[1]	9	74	6	78	H.S. Diloma
COLLEGE	Community Adult Portland, Oregon	MAJOR Business MINOR English	9	78	6	79	N/A
POST GRADUATE, BUSINESS SCHOOL, OR OTHER	N/A						

MILITARY

FROM	TO	BRANCH OF SERVICE N/A	RANK

WHAT IS YOUR PRESENT RESERVE OR DRAFT STATUS?

SPECIALIZED TRAINING OR SCHOOLS ATTENDED

DECORATIONS RECEIVED AND/OR INJURIES SUSTAINED

neat ☐   accurate ☐   complete ☐

2.

SCHOOLS	NAME & LOCATION	COURSES	ATTENDED FROM MO.	YR.	TO MO.	YR.	DEGREE
HIGH OR PREP	Kennedy High School, Portland	ACAD. COMM. VOC. N/A	9	74	6	78	
COLLEGE	Community Adult Portland	MAJOR Business MINOR English	9	78	6	79	
POST GRADUATE, BUSINESS SCHOOL, OR OTHER							

MILITARY

FROM	TO	BRANCH OF SERVICE	RANK

WHAT IS YOUR PRESENT RESERVE OR DRAFT STATUS?

SPECIALIZED TRAINING OR SCHOOLS ATTENDED

DECORATIONS RECEIVED AND/OR INJURIES SUSTAINED

neat ☐   accurate ☐   complete ☐

---

[1] N/A: "not applicable" (this information does not relate to you)

3.

			ATTENDED				
SCHOOLS	NAME & LOCATION	COURSES	FROM		TO		DEGREE
			MO.	YR.	MO.	YR.	
HIGH OR PREP	Kennedy High School Portland, Oregon	ACAD. COMM. VOC. N/A	9	74	6	78	H.S. Diploma
COLLEGE	Community Adult Portland, Oregon	MAJOR Business MINOR English	9	78	6	79	N/A
POST GRADUATE, BUSINESS SCHOOL, OR OTHER	N/A						

EDUCATIONAL RECORD

MILITARY

FROM	TO	BRANCH OF SERVICE	RANK

N/A

WHAT IS YOUR PRESENT RESERVE OR DRAFT STATUS?

SPECIALIZED TRAINING OR SCHOOLS ATTENDED

DECORATIONS RECEIVED AND/OR INJURIES SUSTAINED

neat ☐   accurate ☐   complete ☐

4. Now fill out the form correctly for Susan B. Anthony.

			ATTENDED				
SCHOOLS	NAME & LOCATION	COURSES	FROM		TO		DEGREE
			MO.	YR.	MO.	YR.	
HIGH OR PREP		ACAD. COMM. VOC.					
COLLEGE		MAJOR MINOR					
POST GRADUATE, BUSINESS SCHOOL, OR OTHER							

EDUCATIONAL RECORD

MILITARY

FROM	TO	BRANCH OF SERVICE	RANK

WHAT IS YOUR PRESENT RESERVE OR DRAFT STATUS?

SPECIALIZED TRAINING OR SCHOOLS ATTENDED

DECORATIONS RECEIVED AND/OR INJURIES SUSTAINED

C. Look at three examples from the part of an application form that asks for employment history. After each example, check if it is neat, accurate and complete. Discuss your answers.

1.

EMPLOYMENT RECORD		
NAME OF EMPLOYER (PRESENT OR MOST RECENT) Strelow Co.	ADDRESS 2860 Friendly St., Eugene Ore.	STARTED: DATE 9/79
YOUR POSITION Genral ofice clerk	NAME AND TITLE OF IMMEDIATE SUPERIOR Ms. Erline Dean	SALARY $700/mo.
DESCRIPTION OF DUTIES Typing, filing, ansering phones		LEFT: DATE Present
REASON FOR LEAVING Beter oppty. to avance		SALARY $700/mo.
NAME OF EMPLOYER Russell Insurance Co.	ADDRESS 1300 Main St., Portland	STARTED: DATE 6/79
YOUR POSITION File clerk	NAME AND TITLE OF IMMEDIATE SUPERIOR Mr. George Burns	SALARY $550/mo.
DESCRIPTION OF DUTIES alpabetical and numerical filing		LEFT: DATE 8/79
REASON FOR LEAVING Temporary job		SALARY $550/mo.
NAME OF EMPLOYER	ADDRESS	STARTED: DATE
YOUR POSITION	NAME AND TITLE OF IMMEDIATE SUPERIOR	SALARY
DESCRIPTION OF DUTIES		LEFT: DATE
REASON FOR LEAVING		SALARY

neat ☐   accurate ☐   complete ☐

2.

EMPLOYMENT RECORD		
NAME OF EMPLOYER (PRESENT OR MOST RECENT) Strelow Co.	ADDRESS 2860 Friendly St., Eugene	STARTED: DATE 1979
YOUR POSITION General Office Clerk	NAME AND TITLE OF IMMEDIATE SUPERIOR Dean	SALARY $700
DESCRIPTION OF DUTIES Typing, filing, answering phones		LEFT: DATE Present
REASON FOR LEAVING		SALARY $700
NAME OF EMPLOYER Russell Insurance	ADDRESS 1300 Main, Portland Ore.	STARTED: DATE 6/79
YOUR POSITION File Clerk	NAME AND TITLE OF IMMEDIATE SUPERIOR	SALARY
DESCRIPTION OF DUTIES Alphabetical and numerical filing		LEFT: DATE 8/79
REASON FOR LEAVING Temporary job		SALARY $550
NAME OF EMPLOYER	ADDRESS	STARTED: DATE
YOUR POSITION	NAME AND TITLE OF IMMEDIATE SUPERIOR	SALARY
DESCRIPTION OF DUTIES		LEFT: DATE
REASON FOR LEAVING		SALARY

neat ☐   accurate ☐   complete ☐

3.

NAME OF EMPLOYER (PRESENT OR MOST RECENT) ADDRESS		
Strelow Co. 2860 Friendly St, Eugene Ore.	STARTED: DATE 9/79	
YOUR POSITION General office clerk	NAME AND TITLE OF IMMEDIATE SUPERIOR Ms. Erline Dean	SALARY $700/mo.
DESCRIPTION OF DUTIES Typing, filing, answering phones	LEFT DATE Present	
REASON FOR LEAVING Better opportunity to advance	SALARY $700/mo.	
NAME OF EMPLOYER Russell Insurance Co	ADDRESS 1300 Main St, Portland	STARTED: DATE 6/79
YOUR POSITION File Clerk	NAME AND TITLE OF IMMEDIATE SUPERIOR Mr. George Burns	SALARY $550/700/mo.
DESCRIPTION OF DUTIES Alphabetical and numerical filing	LEFT: DATE 8/79	
REASON FOR LEAVING	SALARY $550/mo.	
NAME OF EMPLOYER	ADDRESS	STARTED:
YOUR POSITION	NAME AND TITLE OF IMMEDIATE SUPERIOR	DATE SALARY
DESCRIPTION OF DUTIES	LEFT:	
REASON FOR LEAVING	DATE SALARY	

neat ☐   accurate ☐   complete ☐

4. **Now fill out this part of the form for Susan B. Anthony.**

NAME OF EMPLOYER (PRESENT OR MOST RECENT) ADDRESS		
YOUR POSITION	NAME AND TITLE OF IMMEDIATE SUPERIOR	STARTED: DATE SALARY
DESCRIPTION OF DUTIES	LEFT:	
REASON FOR LEAVING	DATE SALARY	
NAME OF EMPLOYER	ADDRESS	STARTED:
YOUR POSITION	NAME AND TITLE OF IMMEDIATE SUPERIOR	DATE SALARY
DESCRIPTION OF DUTIES	LEFT:	
REASON FOR LEAVING	DATE SALARY	
NAME OF EMPLOYER	ADDRESS	STARTED:
YOUR POSITION	NAME AND TITLE OF IMMEDIATE SUPERIOR	DATE SALARY
DESCRIPTION OF DUTIES	LEFT:	
REASON FOR LEAVING	DATE SALARY	

D. Fill out this application form for a job you would like to apply for.

Position Desired _____ Salary Desired _____ Referred by _____

LAST NAME	**FIRST**	**MIDDLE**	**SOCIAL SECURITY NO.**	

PERSONAL

PRESENT ADDRESS	**STREET**	**CITY**	**STATE**	**ZIP CODE**	**APT. NO.**	**TELEPHONE NO.**	
						AREA CODE	

ARE YOU A U.S. CITIZEN

YES ☐   NO ☐

HAVE YOU EVER BEEN CONVICTED OF A CRIME

EDUCATIONAL RECORD

SCHOOLS	NAME & LOCATION	COURSES	ATTENDED				DEGREE
			FROM		TO		
			MO.	YR.	MO.	YR.	
HIGH OR PREP		ACAD. COMM. VOC.					
COLLEGE		MAJOR MINOR					
POST GRADUATE, BUSINESS SCHOOL, OR OTHER							

MILITARY

FROM	TO	BRANCH OF SERVICE	RANK

WHAT IS YOUR PRESENT RESERVE OR DRAFT STATUS?

SPECIALIZED TRAINING OR SCHOOLS ATTENDED

DECORATIONS RECEIVED AND/OR INJURIES SUSTAINED

EMPLOYMENT RECORD

NAME OF EMPLOYER (PRESENT OR MOST RECENT)	ADDRESS	STARTED: DATE
YOUR POSITION	NAME AND TITLE OF IMMEDIATE SUPERIOR	SALARY
DESCRIPTION OF DUTIES		LEFT: DATE
REASON FOR LEAVING		SALARY

NAME OF EMPLOYER	ADDRESS	STARTED: DATE
YOUR POSITION	NAME AND TITLE OF IMMEDIATE SUPERIOR	SALARY
DESCRIPTION OF DUTIES		LEFT: DATE
REASON FOR LEAVING		SALARY

NAME OF EMPLOYER	ADDRESS	STARTED: DATE
YOUR POSITION	NAME AND TITLE OF IMMEDIATE SUPERIOR	SALARY
DESCRIPTION OF DUTIES		LEFT: DATE
REASON FOR LEAVING		SALARY

Signature _____   Date _____

E. For more practice, fill out the form on page 120.

Part 2
CAREER GOALS

Objective: To consider how your future plans relate to the job you are applying for

INTRODUCTION

Before you listen to the recording, study the vocabulary below. Then discuss the Focus Questions.

VOCABULARY

1. **definite:** specific or exact
   —He has a *definite* idea about his future. He wants to be a welder.

2. **fit in:** get along well
   —I will *fit in* at this company because I like this kind of work.

3. **goal:** a future plan
   —She's studying medicine. Her *goal* is to become a doctor.

4. **investment:** something that requires money and time to make more money
   —Buying a house is a good *investment*. You can usually sell it for more money in the future.

Focus Questions ——————

A. Why do interviewers ask about your future plans?

B. Does the job you want now relate to the job you want in the future?

EXERCISE 1

Listen to the following conversations about the importance of career goals. Answer the questions after each conversation.

CONVERSATION #1—*Lynn Petersen, the interviewer for an engineering company*

1. What should applicants know about the job they are applying for?

2. Why should applicants have definite career goals?

CONVERSATION #2—*Farhad Samie, the personnel director for a department store*

  3. Why are new employees investments for the company?

  4. How does the interviewer decide if someone will be a good investment?

CONVERSATION #3—*William Harris, from an insurance company*

  5. Why are career goals important to Mr. Harris?

  6. Would he hire someone whose career goals did not relate to the company?

  7. What is he really looking for?

 How important do you think career goals are?

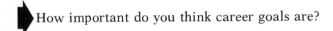

EXERCISE 2

Complete these sentences with a word or a phrase. Some sentences can have more than one answer.

  1. Applicants should know how the job they want will help them in the

     _____ .

  2. Definite career goals help interviewers decide if applicants will
     _____ at the company.

  3. Companies spend a lot of _____ and _____ training
     applicants.

  4. Applicants show they are interested in the job if they have _____ .

EXERCISE 3
Role-Play: Interviewer and Applicant

Sometimes you have to talk about your career goals in an interview.

Look at this interview situation.

What job are you applying for?

I'm applying for the job as a typist.

What are your career goals?

Eventually, I'd like to be a secretary.

Now choose a partner, and practice answering the questions, "What job are you applying for?" and "What are your career goals?" Use the information below.

1. job: service station attendant
   career goals: auto mechanic*

2. job: warehouse worker
   career goals: warehouse foreman [1] *

3. job: waiter
   career goals: restaurant manager*

4. job: general office clerk
   career goals: office supervisor [2] *

5. job: bookkeeper
   career goals: accountant†

6. job: nurse's aide
   career goals: nurse†

7. job: *a job you would like*
   career goals: *your career goals*

NOTE

* These jobs may require more training.
† These jobs require a degree and a certificate.

---

[1] foreman: supervisor
[2] supervisor: the person responsible for a group of workers

Part 3
STABILITY

Objective: To explain your employment record to an interviewer in a positive way

INTRODUCTION

Before you listen to the recording, study the vocabulary below. Then discuss the Focus Questions.

VOCABULARY

1. **attendance:** the act of being at a place
   —You have good *attendance* on the job if you go to work every day.

2. **long-term:** for a long time
   —His last job was *long-term*. He worked for the company for ten years.

3. **punctuality:** the act of being on time
   —*Punctuality* means you always arrive on time.

4. **stability:** the act of being consistent and dependable
   —You show *stability* when you have good attendance and punctuality, and you stay on a job for a long time.

Focus Questions

A. Why do companies want to hire people who will work for them for a long time?

B. What does the length of time you have stayed on past jobs tell the interviewer?

EXERCISE 1

Listen to the following conversations about why stability is important. Answer the questions after each conversation.

CONVERSATION #1—*Kathleen Jackson, the personnel director for a gas and electric company*

1. What kinds of things on past jobs show stability?

2. Why is the interviewer interested in attendance and punctuality on previous jobs?

CONVERSATION #2—*David Sato, an interviewer for a bank*

3. How can the interviewer tell if a person will stay with the company?

4. Why does he want to know the reasons an applicant left a previous job?

▶ What things in your past, besides work experience, show stability?

EXERCISE 2

A.

Interviewers are interested in people with long-term jobs and people with good reasons for leaving jobs.

Read the employment records. Then answer the questions.

JOHN HAMILTON'S APPLICATION FORM — TODAY'S DATE: 11/7/79

EMPLOYMENT RECORD

Company Name and Address	Dates Employed Month Year	Reason for Leaving
Name Sterling Metals	From 4 / 79	Better salary
Address 423 Main St.	To 10 / 79	
Name Label Co.	From 11 / 78	Better salary
Address 134 Second Ave.	To 3 / 79	
Name Barton Mfg. Co.	From 3 / 78	Better salary
Address 99 Oak St.	To 10 / 78	

1. How long did John work for each company?

2. Are these long-term jobs?

3. Why did he leave each company?

▶Do you think his reasons for leaving each job are good?

NELSON LUGO'S APPLICATION FORM—TODAY'S DATE: 3/7/80

EMPLOYMENT RECORD

Company Name and Address	Dates Employed Month Year	Reason for Leaving
Name Janitorial Services **Address** 1632 Market St.	**From** 11 / 78 **To** Present	looking for welding job
Name Housecleaning Co. **Address** 411 Jones St.	**From** 12 / 76 **To** 8 / 77	Returned to school in welding
Name Morton Co. **Address** 32 Grand River	**From** 3 71 **To** 11 / 76	Laid off¹

4. How long has Nelson worked for Janitorial Services?

5. Why does he want to leave?

6. How long did Nelson work for the Housecleaning Company and the Morton Company?

7. After he was laid off from the Morton Company, how long was he without a job?

8. Why was there a gap between August 1977 and November 1978?

▶ Which applicant would you hire, John Hamilton or Nelson Lugo?

---

¹ (was) laid off: lost the job because the company did not have enough work

B.

Interviewers look for good attendance and short gaps between jobs.

Look at the periods of unemployment on the application forms below. Then answer the questions.

BARBARA HENDERSON'S APPLICATION FORM—TODAY'S DATE: 6/2/80

PERIODS OF UNEMPLOYMENT—include all periods of unemployment over 30 days for the last 5 years

FROM	Mo.	Yr.	TO	Mo.	Yr.	REASON
FROM	*1*	*80*	TO	*3*	*80*	REASON *Looking for better job*
FROM	*4*	*78*	TO	*5*	*78*	REASON *Vacation*
FROM	Mo.	Yr.	TO	Mo.	Yr.	REASON

DAYS ABSENT FROM WORK LAST YEAR: *8*

1. What was Barbara doing from January to March, 1980?

2. What was she doing from April to May, 1978?

3. How many days was she absent from work last year?

▶Does she have good reasons for leaving her jobs?

JANET SELINSKY'S APPLICATION FORM—TODAY'S DATE: 3/15/80

PERIODS OF UNEMPLOYMENT—include all periods of unemployment over 30 days for the last 5 years

FROM	Mo.	Yr.	TO	Mo.	Yr.	REASON
FROM	*2*	*80*	TO	*Present*		REASON *Laid off*
FROM	Mo.	Yr.	TO	Mo.	Yr.	REASON
FROM	Mo.	Yr.	TO	Mo.	Yr.	REASON

DAYS ABSENT FROM WORK LAST YEAR: *2*

4. When was Janet laid off from her last job?

5. How many days was she absent from work last year?

▶Which applicant would you hire, Barbara Henderson or Janet Selinsky?

C.

    Fill out the form below. Then choose a partner, and explain your employment record in a positive way. If you have never worked before, explain what you have been doing since you left school.

EMPLOYMENT RECORD

Name & Address of Company	Time Employed From To	Reasons for Leaving

PERIODS OF UNEMPLOYMENT — include all periods of unemployment over 30 days for the last 5 years

FROM	Mo.	Yr.	TO	Mo.	Yr.	REASON
FROM	Mo.	Yr.	TO	Mo.	Yr.	REASON
FROM	Mo.	Yr.	TO	Mo.	Yr.	REASON

DAYS ABSENT FROM WORK LAST YEAR: _____

Part 4

THE QUESTIONS YOU ASK

Objective: To ask the interviewer the right questions to get the information you need

INTRODUCTION

Before you listen to the recording, study the vocabulary below. Then discuss the Focus Questions.

VOCABULARY

1. **particular:**   specific
—He's only interested in one *particular* job.

2. **raise:**   increase in salary at the same company
—He got a $25.00 *raise* after working six months.

3. **sick leave:**   time off that the employer gives when you are sick
—Employees usually get one day of *sick leave* a month.

Focus Questions

A. What questions should you ask the interviewer during an interview?

B. Are there some questions you would not ask?

EXERCISE 1

Listen to the following conversations about asking questions during an interview. Answer the questions after each interviewer's comments.

CONVERSATION #1—*Lynn Petersen, from an engineering company*

1. What are the two most important questions to ask during an interview?

2. What other things should you ask about?

CONVERSATION #2—*John Santoni, the personnel manager of a large hotel*

3. When does the interviewer give you information about raises, sick leave, vacations and benefits?

4. When should an applicant ask these questions?

It is important to ask questions at the right time. What is a good way to ask these questions?

EXERCISE 2

During an interview, the interviewer will usually tell you about:

> the hours   the raises
> the duties   the benefits
> the salary   the opportunities to advance

At the end of the interview, you will have a chance to ask questions. Ask about the things that the interviewer has not already told you.

FOR EXAMPLE:

JOB: *Receptionist*

Interviewer: You'll be working from 8 A.M. to 5 P.M. You'll answer the phone, take messages and do some light typing. Do you have any questions?

Applicant: Yes. What is the starting salary?

The applicant could also ask:
> How often do you give raises?
> What benefits do you offer?
> What are the opportunities to advance?

> NOTE:
> Don't say,
> "When do I get a raise?"
> or
> "What benefits do I get?"

Read what the interviewers have told the applicants for these jobs. Decide what questions each applicant should ask.

1. JOB: *Maintenance person*

   Interviewer: You'll be doing maintenance work, cleaning and repairing equipment. The starting salary is $750 a month. Are there any questions that you want to ask?

   Applicant: _____

2. JOB: *Welder*

   Interviewer: The starting salary is $800 a month, and we give raises every six months. Is there anything else you'd like to know?

   Applicant: _____

3. JOB: *Bookkeeper*

   Interviewer: The salary is $750 a month. You'll get health insurance, one day of sick leave a month and two weeks of vacation each year. Do you have any questions?

   Applicant: _____

4. JOB: *Clerk-typist*

   Interviewer: The benefits include medical and dental insurance, one week of vacation the first year, and two weeks after that. In the future you'll have an opportunity to advance to a job as a secretary. Would you like to ask any questions?

   Applicant: _____

What Are You Going To Say?

Interviewers ask you questions to find out about your qualifications for the job. In this unit you will hear several answers to four difficult questions. If you can answer these questions well, your interview will be much easier.

Part 1

WHAT CAN YOU TELL ME ABOUT YOURSELF?

Objective: To talk about things in your background that relate to the job

INTRODUCTION

Before you listen to the recording, study the vocabulary. Then discuss the Focus Question.

VOCABULARY

1. **background:** education and experience
   —Classes in electronics and experience as a telephone repairman are part of his *background*.

2. **brush up:** go over something you have already learned in order to improve it
   —He hadn't taken dictation in several years, so he's taking a class in shorthand to *brush up*.

3. **to be good at (something):** to do something well
   —She's *good at* math. She's also *good at* working with people.

Focus Question

When interviewers say, "Tell me about yourself," what do they want to know?

EXERCISE 1

An interview sometimes begins with the question, "What can you tell me about yourself?" [1] Interviewers want to know about your qualifications. They are interested in how your background relates to the job. They do not want to know about your personal life.

Listen to the interviews, and answer the questions after each interview.

CONVERSATION #1—*Martha Campbell is applying for a job as a secretary.*

Listen for the questions the interviewer asks her.

1. What does Mrs. Campbell talk about first?

2. What kind of business courses did she take in high school?

3. What were some of her duties on her past jobs?

4. What is she studying now?

Why did the interviewer have to ask her a lot of questions?

CONVERSATION #2—*Donald Thompson is applying for a job as a general office clerk at an insurance company.*

Listen for his qualifications.

5. Does Mr. Thompson say he's qualified for the job?

6. What does the interviewer think when Donald says, "I was just [2] a file clerk"?

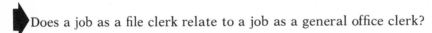Does a job as a file clerk relate to a job as a general office clerk?

CONVERSATION #3—*Roger Kaplan is applying for a job as a mechanic.*

Listen for his qualifications.

7. What did Mr. Kaplan study in high school?

8. What is his job experience?

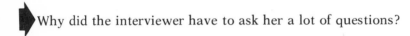Why is this a good answer?

---

[1] Sometimes interviewers say, "Tell me something about your background," or "Can you give me some information about yourself?"

[2] just: only

CONVERSATION #4—*Ellen Lee is applying for a job as a salesperson at a department store.*
Listen to what she says about herself.

   9. Why does Ms. Lee think she would be good at selling?

   10. How does she answer the question, "Do you have any experience selling?" [1]

   ▶ Discuss other ways to answer when you do not have experience for the job you are applying for.

EXERCISE 2

A. Look at your answers to questions 2, 3 and 4 in Exercise 1. Use this information to answer the question, "What can you tell me about yourself?" for Mrs. Campbell.

   1. When I was in high school, I studied _____, _____

   and _____.

   2. I had two jobs before. Some of my duties were _____,

   _____ and _____.

   3. Now I'm studying _____ and _____ for practice.

B. Now complete as many sentences as you can with information about yourself.

   1. When I was in school, I studied _____

   _____

   2. I had _____ jobs before. Some of my duties were _____

   _____

   3. Some of my skills are _____

   _____

   4. I'm good at _____

   _____

   5. I'm studying _____

   _____

   6. Now I'd like to _____

   _____

---

[1] experience selling: Use the *-ing* form of the verb after the word *experience* (experience *using* a calculator, experience *building* cabinets).

EXERCISE 3

Decide which job you would like to apply for. Then make a list of your related education, experience and skills.

FOR EXAMPLE: JOB: CASHIER

EDUCATION	EXPERIENCE	SKILLS
high school math bookkeeping class accounting class	*gen. ofc. clerk - 1 yr. typing, filing, bookkeeping*	*typ. 60 wpm good at figures hard worker*

JOB: _____

EDUCATION	EXPERIENCE	SKILLS

Use the information in your notes and write a paragraph to answer the question, "What can you tell me about yourself?"

FOR EXAMPLE:

I studied math in high school. I liked it a lot, so I took a class in bookkeeping in night school. I worked as a general office clerk for one year. I did typing, filing and bookkeeping. Then I decided to go back to school. I am studying accounting now. I can type 60 wpm. I am good at figures, and I am a hard worker.

_____

_____

_____

_____

EXERCISE 4

Role-Play: Interviewer and Applicant

Choose a partner, and practice answering the questions, "What job are you applying for?" and "What can you tell me about yourself?" As you listen to your partner's answers, take notes.

RELATED EDUCATION: _____

_____

RELATED EXPERIENCE: _____

_____

RELATED SKILLS: _____

_____

Part 2

WHAT ARE YOUR GREATEST STRENGTHS?

Objective: To talk about things that show you are a good worker

INTRODUCTION

Before you listen to the recording, study the vocabulary below. Then discuss your answers to the Focus Questions.

VOCABULARY

1. **catch on:** learn
   —The supervisor is impressed with the new shipping clerk because she *catches on* quickly.

2. **efficient:** able to do things quickly and well
   —A telephone operator has to be *efficient*.

3. **greatest:** best
   —The *greatest* thing about the new employee is that he is assertive.

4. **strengths:** strong points
   —One of her *strengths* is mathematics. She should study to be an accountant.

Focus Questions

A. What are some of your strong points?

B. If you don't have any special skills for a job, what are some other strong points you can talk about?

EXERCISE 1

Interviewers often ask the question, "What are your greatest strengths?" or "What are some of your strong points?" *Strong points* are things that show you would be a good worker. They are the things you do well, and they show the way you work.

Listen to these interviews, and answer the questions after each interview.

CONVERSATION #1—*Harold Edwards is applying for a job as a clerk-typist.*

Listen for the questions the interviewer asks.

1. Why are typing and filing Mr. Edwards' greatest strengths?

▶ Why does the interviewer have to ask a lot of questions?

▶ What do you think of Mr. Edwards' answers?

CONVERSATION #2—*Janice Carter is applying for a job as a health aide.*

    Listen for her strengths.

    2. What are some of her strengths?

    3. How does she answer the question, "Do you have any special skills?"

    ▶ Why is this a good answer?

CONVERSATION #3—*Sue Yamato is applying for a job as a secretary.*

    Listen for her strengths.

    4. How do you know that she is efficient?

    5. How do you know that she is well organized?

    ▶ Why is it good to give examples of your strong points?

EXERCISE 2

When you talk about the way you work, you should give examples that show your strong points.

A. **What are some of the strong points of the students in your class? Make a list of them on the board. Give examples that show the person's strengths.**

B. **Write two sentences that describe you, or choose two sentences below. Add information from your background that shows your strong points.**

    FOR EXAMPLE:

    a. I'm flexible and patient. *On my last job, I did work for three different people. I also trained new employees.*

    b. I'm capable,[1] and I work well with others. *When I was in school, I organized a car wash to make money for the class.*

    1. _____

    _____

    2. _____

    _____

    3. I'm energetic, and I catch on quickly.

    _____

    _____

    4. I'm thorough, and my work is accurate.

    _____

    _____

[1] capable: able to do things well

5. I'm organized, and I work well with others.

_____

_____

6. I'm dependable, and I have a lot of initiative.[1]

_____

_____

7. I'm cooperative, and I work quickly.

_____

_____

8. I'm responsible, and I'm careful when I work.

_____

_____

9. I'm efficient, and I'm a hard worker.

_____

_____

10. I'm capable and patient.

_____

_____

EXERCISE 3

Role-Play: Interviewer and Applicant

Choose a partner, and practice answering the question, "What are your greatest strengths?"

As you listen, list your partner's strong points. Be sure he or she gives examples that explain each strength.

STRONG POINTS	EXAMPLES

[1] initiative: the ability to get things started

Part 3

WHAT DO YOU CONSIDER YOUR WEAKNESSES?

Objective: To answer questions about things you need to improve

INTRODUCTION

Before you listen to the recording, read the paragraph below. Then discuss the Focus Questions.

A *weakness* is something that you do not do well. Everyone does some things better than other things. You need to know your strengths, but you also need to know your weaknesses.

Focus Questions

A. What things are difficult for you?

B. What could you do to improve each one?

EXERCISE 1

Interviewers sometimes ask about your weaknesses. A good answer tells what you are doing to improve a skill you are weak in. Some people cannot think of any weaknesses. The interviewer might think that these people do not know very much about themselves.

Listen to the interviews, and answer the questions after each interview.

CONVERSATION #1—*Matthew Kelly is applying for a job as a cashier.*

Listen to his answers.

1. How is Mr. Kelly's math?

2. What is he doing to improve it?

CONVERSATION #2—*Teresa Ortiz is applying for a job as a clerk-typist.*

Listen to her answer to the question, "How are your spelling and punctuation?"

3. What is she doing to improve her punctuation?

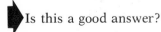 Is this a good answer?

CONVERSATION #3—*Donna Reed is applying for a job as a printer.*

Listen to her answer the question, "Do you have any weaknesses?"

4. What is Donna's weakness?

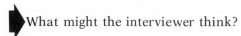 What might the interviewer think?

CONVERSATION #4—*Alex Bell is applying for a job as a file clerk.*

Listen to his answer.

5. What is Mr. Bell's weakness?

6. What is he doing to improve it?

Why is this a good answer?

EXERCISE 2

If you talk about your weaknesses, you should always tell the interviewer what you are doing to improve them.

FOR EXAMPLE:

"I need to improve in *math*, so I'm *taking a class in it*." Practice saying, "I need to improve in _____, so I'm _____." Use the information below.

1. English
2. TV repair
3. foreign car repair
4. typing
5. spelling
6. punctuation
7. shorthand
8. using a lathe
9. using a calculator
10. (*your weakness*)   (*what you are doing to improve*)

> **NOTE**
> An interviewer might ask, "Do you have any weaknesses?" It is not necessary to say, "Yes, I do." It is better to talk about what you need to improve, as in the example.

EXERCISE 3

Role-Play: Interviewer and Applicant

Choose a partner, and practice answering the question, "What are your weaknesses?" As you listen to your partner's answer, take notes.

What is your partner doing to improve them?

_____

_____

_____

What are your partner's weaknesses?

_____

_____

_____

Part 4

WHAT ARE YOUR CAREER GOALS?

Objective: To relate your future plans to the job

INTRODUCTION

Before you listen to the recording, study the vocabulary below. Then discuss the Focus Questions.

VOCABULARY

management: the work of a manager
                    —He's applying for an entry-level job.
                    Eventually he'd like to work in *management*.

Focus Questions

A. What would you like to do in the future?

B. How do you plan to reach your goals?

EXERCISE 1

As you learned in Unit 5, interviewers want to know about your career goals.

Some applicants want to move up to a higher position (for example, from general office work to management). Other applicants plan to go back to school. Some people are not sure about their career goals. But in an interview you should always say something about your future. Remember that interviewers like definite career goals that relate to the job you are applying for.

Listen to the interviews, and answer the questions after each interview.

CONVERSATION #1—*Cindy Ruiz is applying for a job as a bookkeeper.*

Listen to her plans for the future.

1. What does Ms. Ruiz plan to do in the future?

2. Is this related to the job as a bookkeeper?

Does she sound interested in the job she is applying for?

CONVERSATION #2—*Glen Robinson is applying for a job as a mail clerk.*

Listen to his answers.

3. What are Mr. Robinson's future plans?

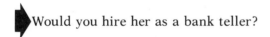What is wrong with his answer?

CONVERSATION #3—*Mary Allen is applying for a job as a bank teller.*

Listen for her career goals.

4. What does Ms. Allen really want to be?

Would you hire her as a bank teller?

CONVERSATION #4—*Peter Haas is applying for a job as a shipping clerk.*

Listen for his career goals.

5. What does Mr. Haas eventually hope to do?

6. How does he plan to get there?

Did he give a good answer? Why or why not?

EXERCISE 2

A. The chart below shows the different departments of the Cook Company. Read the chart to find out how the company is organized.

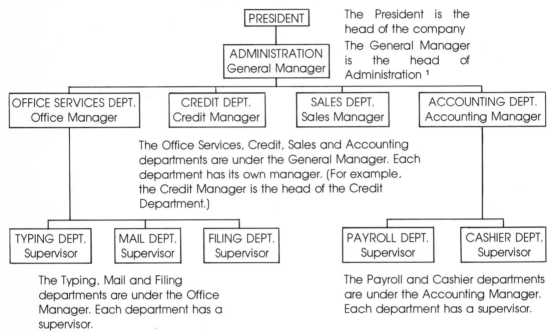

The President is the head of the company

The General Manager is the head of Administration [1]

The Office Services, Credit, Sales and Accounting departments are under the General Manager. Each department has its own manager. (For example, the Credit Manager is the head of the Credit Department.)

The Typing, Mail and Filing departments are under the Office Manager. Each department has a supervisor.

The Payroll and Cashier departments are under the Accounting Manager. Each department has a supervisor.

Now answer the questions.

1. Who has the highest position in the company?

2. Who has more responsibility, the General Manager or the Credit Manager?

3. Can an employee in the Payroll Department move up to the Accounting Department?

4. Can an employee in the Sales Department move up to be the General Manager?

5. If you work in the Mail Department, can you move up to the Credit Department?

6. If you work in the Typing Department, what departments can you move up to?

---

[1] Administration: the people who are responsible for the management of a company

B. **If you apply for a job at the Cook Company, what can you say about your career goals? Use the chart, and say: "Eventually I'd like to work in (*the name of a department*)."**

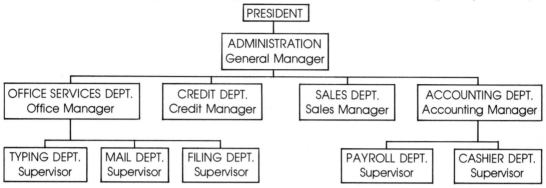

Complete the sentences.

FOR EXAMPLE:

If you apply for a job in the Payroll Department, you can say: "Eventually I'd like to work *in the Accounting Department.*"

1. If you apply for a job in the Filing Department, say:

_____

2. If you apply for a job in the Credit Department, say:

_____

3. If you apply for a job in the Cashier Department, say:

_____

4. If you apply for a job in the Office Services Department, say:

_____

5. If you apply for a job in the Typing Department, say:

_____

EXERCISE 3

Role-Play: Interviewer and Applicant

Choose a partner, and practice answering the questions, "What job are you applying for?" and "What are your career goals?" As you listen, take notes. Do your partner's career goals relate to the job that he or she is applying for?

Job: _____

Career goals: _____

_____

_____

_____

ANSWER KEY

Unit Two

PART 3 / EXERCISE 3

1. **WAITRESS**—sets the tables, takes food orders, brings the food to the table.
   RESTAURANT MANAGER—directs the work in the dining room, plans the workers' hours, talks to customers about problems.

2. **AUTO MECHANIC**—fixes motors, decides what to repair, buys automobile parts.
   SERVICE STATION ATTENDANT—checks the oil, washes the car windows, pumps gas.

3. **SECRETARY**—writes and types letters, makes appointments, organizes the work of the file clerk.
   FILE CLERK—puts folders in alphabetical and numerical order, pulls folders from the files, puts labels on folders.

PART 4 / EXERCISE 2

1. a. Both take care of people and give first aid.
   b. Both deal with medical records.
   c. Both are concerned with health.

2. a. Both work with numbers.
   b. Both work in an office.
   c. Both are responsible for finances.

3. a. Both repair electrical systems.
   b. Both repair electrical systems.
   c. Both know about electronic equipment.

4. a. Both have to convince people.
   b. Both deal with people.
   c. Both do paper work, and have desk jobs.

Unit Three

PART 3 / EXERCISE 3

	TYPE OF CO.	F/T or P/T	DUTIES	SALARY OR WAGE	HOURS	BENEFITS	OPPORTUNITIES
1. SERVICE STATION ATTENDANT Exp. req. Full time $3.25/hr. night shift. Shell-corner Fell & Baker.	✓	✓		✓	✓		
2. RECEPTIONIST for dental ofc. 4-day wk. answer phones. good benefits. Write to this paper. Ad no. 17294.	✓	✓				✓	
3. ACCOUNTING CLERK for small insurance office. Exp. pref. Gd. salary. Room to advance. 435-0946	✓			✓		✓	✓

PART 3 / EXERCISE 4

	INFORMATION ABOUT JOB	REQUIREMENTS	PREFERRED QUALIFICATIONS
1. CLERK TYPIST M/F for airlines. Must be able to type 65 wpm accurately and work afternoon shift. 1 yr. clerical exper. Call 788-8100, ext. 225	airlines afternoon shift	typ. 65 wpm 1 yr. clerical exp.	
2. MACHINE REPAIR Must have exp. electrical knowledge preferred. Sm. TV-Stereo company 14 Mile Road. Call Barbara 585-8220 for appt.	sm. TV-Stereo co.	exp.	elec. knowledge

3.
MAINTENANCE MECHANIC Must have exp. in repair of equip., work in electrical repair pref. Must have own hand tools. Sheldon Transport Company, 17011 Beaumont, Salt Lake City, Utah 84112

exp. repair equip. own hand tools — *elec. repair*

4.
MECHANIC—exp. in bldg. repairs. .Knowledge of elec. tools helpful, gd. sal. & ben. Engineering company 52 First St., Cambridge 547-2700

gd. sal. + ben. engineer co. — *exp. bldg. repairs* — *Knowledge elec. tools*

5.
OFFICE MGR. for doctor's office. Bilingual Spanish/English. Good telephone manner.¹ 8-5 P.M. 648-6066.

dr.'s ofc. — *bil. Sp/Eng. gd. phone manner*

6.
PAINTERS HELPER wanted.² No exp. required. Start $4.30 hr. 960-8614

$4.30/hr.

7.
RECEPTIONIST Answer busy phones, meet public, type letters, other office duties. Good phone manner and typing required. Min. 1 year office exper. Good salary & benefits. CITY SAVINGS & LOAN 700 Market St. 772-1481.

answer busy phones meet public + typ. letters - gd. sal. + ben. — *gd. phone manner typ.* — *1 yr. ofc. exp.*

8.
SECRETARY—full time, 10-6 M-F. Must type 65 wpm. Some office exp. preferred. Ask for Susan 527-8047

F/T 10-6, M-F — *typ. 65 wpm* — *some ofc. exp.*

9.
SERVICE STATION Attendant—1 yr. exper. 5 days 40 hrs. Tues-Sat. Apply at Union Oil, 300 W. Portal Ave. San Francisco

service station 5 days, 40 hrs. Tues. - Sat. — *1 yr. exp.*

10.
WELDER Move to beautiful Vermont. Good benefits & working cond. Min. 5 yrs. exp. Call 802 689-5034 or write to Route 1, Brattleboro, Vt. 05301

gd. ben. + wk. conditions — *5 yrs. exp.*

Unit Four

PART 2 / EXERCISE 4

Dental Asst.
Service Station Attendant
Hair Stylist
Davids Agency
Secretary

Unit Five

PART 2 / EXERCISE 2

1. future
2. fit in
3. time, money
4. career goals

Unit Six

PART 4 / EXERCISE 2

1. The President.
2. The General Manager.
3. Yes.
4. Yes.
5. Yes.
6. Office Services, Credit, Sales or Accounting.

TRANSCRIPT

Unit Two

PART 1 / The Hours You Work

EXERCISE 1, page 15

—Mark, why do you work nights?

—Well, that's when a lot of keypunch operators work. They begin working nights, and that's when most of the work is done. Eventually, I'll be able to move up and change my shift.

—Uh huh . . . Well, how do you like working nights?

—It's not so bad. I enjoy it. I plan to stay in this field. I was offered a job doing office work during the day, but I prefer doing what I was trained for. So that's why I took a job at night.

PART 2 / Job Security

EXERCISE 1, page 18

—Why did you accept this job?

—Well, it's a place where I knew I could work for several years. The company's getting bigger, and they told me there was always going to be a need for welders. Actually, I applied for a job with a better salary and benefits, and they wanted to hire me . . .

—Oh, well, why didn't you take that job?

—Well, it would only last for about one and a half to two years, and I just didn't want to do that. I really need a job with some security.

PART 3 / Making Decisions

EXERCISE 1, page 20

—What do you do here at the factory?

—Well, I'm responsible for keeping the machines in good working order. I have to look and see if any problems are coming up and take care . . . before they get serious. I repair the machines when they break down.

—Uh huh . . . Now, tell me. You had a different job before this.

—Yes.

—Now, how is this job different from the last one you had?

—Well, on this job there's a lot more responsibility. I have to make all the decisions myself. To tell the truth, I almost didn't take the job because of that.

—Why? Were you a little frightened about it?

—Yes. I was a little bit afraid of making a lot of decisions.

—Uh huh . . . Well, are you glad you did?

—Very glad. In the old job, it was nice because it was comfortable. You know, there were always people to tell you what to do and how to fix things. You know, like that. But, . . . and I never had any real problems. But . . . I didn't have to make the decisions. And now, this job, because I have to make the decisions, it's a lot more interesting. To tell the truth, I'm really glad I took a chance.

PART 4 / Changing Fields

EXERCISE 1, page 23

—Francisco, what did you do before you took this job with the bank?

—Well, actually, I taught elementary school in Colombia. And I decided to move to the United States and when I got here, I started to look for work. I did this for six months. I realized that it was going to be very hard, and I really needed to make some money.

—I imagine. What kind of a job were you looking for?

—Well, first of all, I was looking for a job as a teacher. I realized that it was not going to be possible for me to work as a teacher in this country because I didn't have a teaching certificate. A friend of mine told me about an entry-level job at the bank. It seemed to me that it was an interesting job, basically because I would be working with people, and as you know, a teacher works with people every day.

—Right, right. Is this a temporary job, or do you see it as a new career for you?

—Well, I see it as a start of a new career for me. I've improved a lot on the job so far. I started off as a file clerk and I'm now doing general office work, which is one step above. And, the job just has more responsibility and I like that.

Unit Four

PART 1 / Beginning the Call

EXERCISE 1 · WHO TO ASK FOR, page 48

CALL #1

—Good morning. Reliance Electric.

—Yes. May I speak to Joan, please?

—This is Joan speaking.

CALL #2

—Bob's Auto Shop. May I help you?

—May I speak to Mr. Baker, please?

—Just a minute, please.

—Bob Baker.

CALL #3

—Good afternoon. Red Carpet Realty.

—Yes. Extension 19, please.

—Thank you.

—Personnel. Susan speaking.

CALL #4

—Atlantic Medical Center.

—Could I have extension 31, please?

—One moment, I'll connect you.

—Yes. May I help you?

CALL #5

—United Pacific and Reliance. Good afternoon.

—Good afternoon. The personnel department, please.

—Personnel department? One moment.

—Personnel.

CALL #6

—Appliance Parts Distributors.

—Could I have the personnel department, please?

—Mr. Spencer isn't in right now. Could you call back in about an hour?

—Sure. Thank you.

PART 1 /

EXERCISE 2 · WHAT TO SAY, page 49

1. *When the ad gives the name of a person:*
   a. May I speak to Barbara, please?
   b. May I speak to Ms. Jones, please?

2. *When the ad gives an extension number:*
   a. Could I have extension 31, please?
   b. Extension 31, please.

3. *When the ad gives only a telephone number or says, "Personnel Department":*
   a. Could I have the personnel department, please?
   b. Personnel department, please.

PART 2 / Talking to the Receptionist

EXERCISE 1 · WHAT A RECEPTIONIST MIGHT ASK, page 52

1. —Pennsylvania Parts. Jack speaking.
—Hello. Could I have the personnel department?
—We don't have a personnel department. What are you calling about, please?
—I'm calling about the job as a warehouse assistant.
—OK. Hang on a second.
—Small speaking.

2. —981-6212.
—Yes. Could I have the personnel department, please?
—Personnel? Yes. Who's calling, please?
—This is Harold Edwards.
—Thank you. One moment, please.
—Thank you.
—Yes. Can I help you?

PART 3 / Introducing Yourself

EXERCISE 1 · THREE THINGS TO SAY, page 57

CALL #1
—Good morning. Reliance Electric.
—Yes. May I speak to Joan, please?
—This is Joan speaking.
—This is Mary Johnson. I'm calling about the job as a clerk-typist. I read about it in today's paper.

CALL #2
—Hello. Personnel Department. May I help you?
—Mr. McDonald?
—Yes . . . speaking.
—I heard you have a job opening.
—Yes, we have several. Which job are you talking about?
—The one as a secretary. They told me you needed a secretary.
—Who told you we needed a secretary?
—The agency.
—Well, fine, but we use a lot of different agencies. And what's your name, anyway? I've been expecting several people to call.

CALL #3
—Harry's Auto Shop.
—Can I speak to Harry, please?
—Just a minute, please.
—Hello. Can I help you?
—Yes. This is Bill Anderson, and I'm interested in the job as a mechanic. I was referred by the State Employment Agency.

PART 4 / Giving Your Qualifications

EXERCISE 1 · AFTER THE INTRODUCTION, page 61

1. —Good morning. May I help you?
—Yes. May I speak to Marsha, please?
—Speaking.
—My name is Steve Davis, and I read about your job as a clerk-typist in today's paper.
—Uh huh . . . Can you tell me a little about yourself?
—I can type 50 words a minute and it's accurate, and I have three years' experience working in an office.
—And are you working now, Steve?
—Not in an office position, but I'd like to get back into office work.

2. —D & D Cycles.
—I'm calling about the job as a mechanic.

—OK. Just a second.
—Yeah, Mark speaking.
—Hello. My name is Tom Jones. I'm interested in the job as a mechanic that I saw in today's paper.
—Uh huh . . .
—I worked on Hondas for a few years when I was in high school. I was also taking a class in auto mechanics at that time. I have some experience working on bicycles too.

EXERCISE 3 · A REVIEW OF THE WORDS TO USE, page 70

1. —What are your qualifications?
—I can type 60 words a minute. I can use a dictaphone, and I can do filing.

2. —What qualifications do you have for the job?
—I have four years' carpentry experience, and I can use electrical tools. I've never built cabinets, but I learn quickly.

3. —What are your qualifications for the job?
—I have one year's experience as a bookkeeper. I studied accounting in school, and I'm good with figures.

4. —What are your qualifications?
—I have three years' experience as an auto mechanic. I studied welding in school, and I have my own tools.

5. —What are your qualifications?
—I am a high school graduate, and I can do light typing. I don't have experience as a cashier, but I'd like to learn.

PART 5 / Making the Appointment

EXERCISE 1 · THE INFORMATION YOU NEED TO GET, page 73

A. —OK, fine, Steve. When could you come in for an interview? We have several positions that might be of interest to you.
—Let's see . . . any time tomorrow morning . . .
—OK. How about 10:30?
—That would be fine. That's 10:30 tomorrow, March 15th.
—Good. Do you know where we're located?
—No. What's your address, please?
—52 Second Street.
—That's 52 Second Street. And what are the cross streets?
—It's between Washington and Main.
—That's between Washington and Main.
—Right.
—And who should I ask for?
—Ask for Marsha Carr.
—C-A-R?
—No, it's C-A- double R.
—That's C-A- double R.
—Uh huh . . .
—Great. That's 10:30 tomorrow morning. I'll see you then.
—Yes.
—Thank you very much.
—You're welcome. Goodbye.
—Bye.

B. —I see. Would it be possible to come in for an interview?
—Yes, it would. How about 3 o'clock, Thursday the 10th?
—Fine. Uh huh . . . That's 3 on Thursday, April 10th?
—Right.
—And could you tell me where you're located?
—140 State Street.

—140 State Street.
—Uh huh . . .
—And should I ask for you?
—Yes. My name is Harry Lanzano.
—How do you spell the last name?
—L-A-N . . .
—L-A-N . . .
—Z-A-N-O.
—Z-A-N-O. L-A-N-Z-A-N-O.
—All right . . . fine. Do you know where 140 State Street is?
—No. Could you tell me what the cross streets are?
—Yes. Grant Avenue and Jackson.
—Grant and Jackson.
—Yeah, it's right downtown.
—Great. Well, I'll see you at 3 on Thursday then.
—All right.
—Oh, and thank you.

EXERCISE 2 · WRITING DOWN THE IN-FORMATION, page 74
—How about 4 o'clock on Monday, the 8th?
—OK. That's 4 P.M., Monday, May 8th.
You write: 4 P.M. Monday May 8.

1. —How about 9:30 in the morning?
   —Fine. That's 9:30 A.M.
2. —Is Thursday, July 13th convenient?
   —Uh huh . . . that's Thursday, July 30th.
   —No, July 13th.
   —Oh, I'm sorry. July 13th. OK.
3. —Could you come in Tuesday, August 10th at 4?
   —Yes, fine. That's Tuesday, August 10th at 4 o'clock.
4. —The address is 420 Lake Street.
   —That's 420 Lake Street.
5. —We're at 19 West 44th Street, on the 12th floor.
   —I'm sorry . . . could you repeat that?
   —Sure. That's 19 West 44th Street, on the 12th floor.
   —That's 19 West 44th Street, 12th floor.
6. —We're between Fifth and Sixth Avenue.
   —That's between Fifth and Sixth.
7. —It's on the corner of Post and Grant.
   —Uh huh . . . on the corner of Post and Grant.
8. —My name is David Moore.
   —That's David Moore. M-O-O-R-E?
   —Right.
9. —Ask for Mrs. Bailey.
   —That's Mrs. Bailey. How do you spell that, please?
   —B-A-I . . .
   —B-A-I . . .
   —L-E-Y.
   —L-E-Y.
10. —Ask for Mary Griffin.
    —That's Mary Griffin. How do you spell your last name?
    —G-R-I- double F-I-N.
    —G-R-I-F-F-I-N.

Unit Five
PART 1 / Application Forms
EXERCISE 1, page 83

Conversation #1—Harriet Miller, a personnel interviewer for a bank
—An application form tells me a lot about the applicant. If there are misspelled words, this tells me about their writing ability. They should look for mistakes before handing in the application form.

Some errors show that they just didn't understand the question.
—Well, would this stop you from hiring the applicant?
—Well, a lot of positions at our bank require detail. If they can't handle the detail on an application form, I'm not sure they'll be able to handle the detail on the job.

Conversation #2—Marie Dumas, the personnel director for an electronics manufacturing company
—One of the things I look at closely is the application form. Is it complete, is it neat? Have the applicants read the instructions carefully and then followed them correctly? Have they answered all the questions and not left anything blank? Have they explained any gaps in their employment record?
—Well, what do you do when the form is incomplete?
—I ask them to complete it. But it makes me feel they're not really prepared for the interview. It's better to ask about anything you don't understand on the form before handing it in.

Conversation #3—William Harris, the personnel director for a large insurance company
—Well, one of the first things that impress me is an applicant that is prepared in every way. This really becomes clear in their application forms. They should be filled out correctly as far as dates of past jobs, the addresses of previous employers, their job duties, supervisors' names. In general, all numbers such as a Social Security number and dates should be correct.
—Well, what if an applicant leaves questions unanswered, or numbers and dates are incorrect?
—Well, we can't always interview all the applicants who apply. So the persons who don't complete their application forms might not get an interview.

PART 2 / Career Goals
EXERCISE 1, page 91

Conversation #1—Lynn Petersen, the interviewer for an engineering company
—Well, an applicant should know how the job they are applying for will help them in the future. You know, they should have an idea of how this job will help them get a better job.
—I see.
—If they have definite career goals, it is much easier for me to see if they will fit in here. It seems to me, if they know what they want in their future, they probably know what they want now. And so I know they'll be happy here.

Conversation #2—Farhad Samie, the personnel director for a department store
—Well, quite frankly, we look at the people that we're hiring as investments for our company, for the store. And we spend a great amount of time and money in training these people. So, we want them to think about the future. For many people this is a very, very difficult thing to do, but we expect these people that we train and hire to be working for us for a long, long time.
—Well, how is it that you decide whether or not they are going to be a good investment?
—Well, it's not easy, but it depends upon the way they answer the questions that we ask them. We ask them these questions to have them look to see how they themselves will be in, perhaps, five years' time. The best employees are those who have goals for themselves for the future, and I know that they have a real interest in this job if they themselves have an idea of what they want to do in the future.

Conversation #3—William Harris, from an insurance company
—Well, career goals are very important to me. I want my employees to be happy and stay a long time.
—Well, would you hire someone whose goals didn't relate to your company?
—Well, if they wanted to be a teacher or nurse or something like that, and they are really honest about staying and working hard for three or four years while they study, I possibly would hire them. But I prefer to hire someone whose goals relate directly to the job. Yeah, I'm really looking for permanent employees.

PART 3 / Stability
EXERCISE 1, page 94

Conversation #1—Kathleen Jackson, the personnel director for a gas and electric company
—A person's stability in the past is the most important thing to me. I look for long-term jobs with little or no gaps between jobs. This shows stability in the future.
—Well, are there any other things that show stability?
—Yes. I'm very interested in their attendance and punctuality on their previous jobs. How often were they absent? How often were they late? How they did on past jobs really helps me to know if they will be dependable workers.

Conversation #2—David Sato, the interviewer for a bank
—Primarily, we look for stability in a person. I don't want to hire someone who's going to quit after just a few months.
—Well, how can you tell whether or not a person's going to stay with your company?
—Usually, I can tell by what an applicant has done in the past. I really feel the past tells a lot about the future. So I look over, very carefully, their last four years of work to see how they've been doing and how long they stayed on that previous job. If they've changed jobs a lot, I want to find out why.
—But what if they've had good reasons for, say, leaving that job?
—Well, that's OK, that's fine. But I still want to know the reasons why they left, because if I know why they left a job, I have a pretty good idea of whether they'll stay at this job.

PART 4 / The Questions You Ask
EXERCISE 1, page 99

Conversation #1—Lynn Petersen, from an engineering company
—It impresses me when applicants ask about the opportunities to advance. This shows they're interested in this particular job, and that they're interested in the company. Well, it's also very important for them to ask about the job duties. Those are the two most important things to ask.
—Are there other questions that are good to ask?
—Yeah. They should ask about the hours, the benefits, what the starting salary is. Those are all good questions to ask.

Conversation #2—John Santoni, the personnel manager of a large hotel
—Well, sometimes applicants ask me immediately about raises, sick leave, vacations and benefits before I've even started the interview. That's not a good idea.
—Well, why?
—I always give them that information at the end of the interview, after we've discussed everything else.
—Well, are you saying they shouldn't ask these questions?
—Oh, no, no! It's fine to ask these things at the end of the interview. But if a person starts asking these questions immediately, I really wonder if they're interested in the job, or only in the benefits of the company.

Unit Six

PART 1 / What Can You Tell Me About Yourself?
EXERCISE 1, page 102

Conversation #1—Martha Campbell is applying for a job as a secretary. Listen to the questions the interviewer asks her.
—Martha, tell me a little about your background.
—Well, I'm married and my husband is an electrician. I have two children . . . Katie is 5 and Brad is 7, so they're both in school now. I've been out of work for five years since Katie was born. And I'm trying to get back into the business world again.
—OK . . . Now, what about your education?
—Well, I took business courses in high school.
—What kind of business courses?
—Oh, typing, bookkeeping, math . . .
—Well, could you tell me a little about your work experience?
—Well, I had two jobs before, both of them involved a lot of typing and filing, making appointments, which of course means using the phone, and I did a lot of bookkeeping.
—How are your office skills now?
—Oh, really good. I'm taking typing and business math at school now, brushing up, for practice.

Conversation #2—Donald Thompson is applying for a job as a general office clerk. Listen for his qualifications.
—OK, Mr. Thompson, what can you tell me about yourself?
—Well, I grew up back East. I graduated from high school there. I only had one job before I moved out here. Then, let's see . . . I worked at State Farm Insurance, but I was laid off last month, and that's why I'm applying for this job as a general office clerk.
—Well, what did you do for State Farm?
—I was just a file clerk.
—So then you've never done general office work?
—No, not really.

Conversation #3—Roger Kaplan is applying for a job as a mechanic. Listen for his qualifications.
—Can you give me some information about yourself, Roger?
—Well, I studied mechanics in high school. I did pretty well in it, and I really enjoyed it.
—Uh huh . . .
—I rebuilt foreign and domestic car engines. I fixed all the machines in the school after a while. I had a lot of experience doing repair work on cars, and for me that was important, the experience itself.
—And I see you've had some job experience.
—Well, actually, it was three years' experience in a garage as an assistant mechanic. During the last year, I did almost everything by myself. I feel I really learned a lot, and it's been very valuable to me.

Conversation #4—Ellen Lee is applying for a job as a salesperson at a department store. Listen to what she says about herself.

—Tell me a little about yourself.
—I came to this country four years ago. While I was working as a housekeeper, I was studying English. And now I feel my English is good enough to work with people. I get along well with people. I enjoy selling, and well, I consider all these qualities the most important things for the job.
—But do you have any experience selling?
—No, but I learn quickly, and I think I'll be good at it.

PART 2 / What Are Your Greatest Strengths?
EXERCISE 1, page 105

Conversation #1—Harold Edwards is applying for a job as a clerk-typist. Listen for the questions the interviewer asks.
—Tell me, Mr. Edwards, what do you consider your greatest strengths?
—Let's see . . . typing and filing and . . .
—Well, can you tell me a little more? Why are your typing and filing your greatest strengths?
—I like to type, and I'm good at filing. I try to do the best I can.
—How many words a minute can you type?
—About 55 words a minute . . . 55 or 50.
—Without mistakes? 55 words a minute?
—Yeah, fairly correct.
—And filing? What kind of filing have you done?
—Alphabetical and numerical.
—How long did you study typing and filing?
—Let's see . . . the filing about four months and typing about a year. I'm not sure.

Conversation #2—Janice Carter is applying for a job as a health aide. Listen for her strengths.
—OK, Janice, now, what are your greatest strengths?
—You mean, what am I good at?
—Uh huh . . .
—Well, I enjoy working with people. I worked with a lot of people when I was a cook at a school cafeteria, and I liked that job very much. I am also a hard worker. I got my first job when I was 14, and I've always been dependable.
—Uh huh . . . Now, do you have any special skills?
—Well, I don't have any experience as a health aide, but I catch on very quickly, and I'm sure I'll like the job.

Conversation #3—Sue Yamato is applying for a job as a secretary. Listen to what she says about her strong points.
—What are some of your strong points?
—I'm very efficient. I worked for two years in a very busy office where it was very important that I do things on time. I type 70 words a minute with no errors, correctly. And during those two years, I learned how to run several business machines.
—Do you have any other strengths?
—I had to be very well organized on this job. I was typing for four different people, and I had to be sure that I did the work on time and that I sent it to the right place. And it was very important that I kept my desk organized because I had so much work to do.

PART 3 / What Do You Consider Your Weaknesses?
EXERCISE 1, page 108

Conversation #1—Matthew Kelly is applying for a job as a cashier. Listen to his answers.
—You're going to have to use a lot of math on the job. How is your math?
—I guess it's okay. It's just that I can't do my division very well.
—Are you doing anything to improve it?
—Well, I hadn't thought about it.

Conversation #2—Teresa Ortiz is applying for a job as a clerk-typist. Listen to her answer to the question, "How are your spelling and punctuation?"
—Your typing seems fine. How are your spelling and punctuation?
—My spelling's pretty good. I think I still need to work on punctuation though. I have a book and I'm studying it at home.

Conversation #3—Donna Reed is applying for a job as a printer. Listen to her answer the question, "Do you have any weaknesses?"
—I see you've had good training and some experience. Let's see . . . do you have any weakness?
—No, none that I can think of. No, I can't think of any.

Conversation #4—Alex Bell is applying for a job as a file clerk. Listen to his answer.
—Mr. Bell, what would you say your weaknesses are?
—Probably my typing. But I'm taking a class at night that's really helping.

PART 4 / What Are Your Career Goals?
EXERCISE 1, page 110

Conversation #1—Cindy Ruiz is applying for a job as a bookkeeper. Listen to her plans for the future.
—What do you want to be doing five years from now, Cindy?
—Well, I'm planning to go to college to study accounting.
—Do you plan to continue working full time, or do you want just a part-time job while you're going to school?
—Oh no, I'm looking for a full-time job.
—And then when you start school, will you continue working full time?
—Yes, I will.
—Do you think you'll have the energy, I mean, to go to school and work at the same time?
—Oh, yes! Because when I want to do something, I do it, and I think that if I go to college and study accounting, then I'm going to have better opportunities in the future.

Conversation #2—Glen Robinson is applying for a job as a mail clerk. Listen to his answers.
—What are your future plans? What do you eventually want to do . . . let's say in 5 or 10 years?
—Oh, I really don't know. I'm not sure.
—You're not sure. But do you think that you'll be working?
—Oh, yes, I'll be working for sure, but I don't know what I'm going to be.

Conversation #3—Mary Allen is applying for a job as a bank teller. Listen for her career goals.
—Ms. Allen, what are your plans for the future, say 5 years from now?
—Five years from now? Oh, then I might be teaching. I'd really like to be a teacher.
—Oh. Do you plan to go back to school?
—No, I already have a teaching certificate. I just can't find a job as a teacher.

Conversation #4—Peter Haas is applying for a job as a shipping clerk. Listen for his career goals.
—Do you see yourself as a shipping clerk in the future?
—Well, I think it's a good place to start and a good place to learn about the company. I hope to move up to management eventually.
—How long do you think that'll take?
—Several years, at least.
—How do you plan to get there?
—I'd like to learn as much as I can about the different jobs in the company first. I think if I work hard and learn a lot about the company, that will help.

DOT METAL, INC.

9 West 44th Street, N.Y., N.Y. 10036

LAST NAME	FIRST NAME	MIDDLE	DATE OF APPLICATION / /
ADDRESS			SOCIAL SECURITY NUMBER
CITY	STATE	ZIP	
(A/C) HOME PHONE	(A/C) BUSINESS PHONE	(A/C) MESSAGE PHONE	

EMPLOYMENT RECORD — LAST POSITION FIRST

FIRM NAME 1		TYPE CO.	START SAL. $	MAJOR DUTIES	REASON LEFT
ADDRESS		JOB TITLE	LAST SAL. $		
CITY, STATE		SUPERVISOR'S NAME			
ZIP	PHONE	SUPERVISOR'S TITLE	FROM TO		
FIRM NAME 2		TYPE CO.	START SAL. $	MAJOR DUTIES	REASON LEFT
ADDRESS		JOB TITLE	LAST SAL. $		
CITY, STATE		SUPERVISOR'S NAME			
ZIP	PHONE	SUPERVISOR'S TITLE	FROM TO		
FIRM NAME 3		TYPE CO.		MAJOR DUTIES	REASON LEFT
ADDRESS		JOB TITLE			
CITY, STATE		SUPERVISOR'S NAME			
ZIP		SUPERVISOR'S TITLE	FROM TO		

EDUCATION RECORD

GRADUATE SCHOOL OR OTHER	YR. GRAD	DEGREE	MAJOR	EXTRA CURRICULAR
ADDRESS	GRADE AVG.			
COLLEGE	YR. GRAD	DEGREE	MAJOR	EXTRA CURRICULAR
ADDRESS	GRADE AVG.			
BUSINESS SCHOOL	YR. GRAD	DEGREE	MAJOR	EXTRA CURRICULAR
ADDRESS	GRADE AVG			
HIGH SCHOOL	YR. GRAD	DEGREE	MAJOR	EXTRA CURRICULAR
	GRADE AVG			

HONORS / OTHER EDUCATIONAL ACTIVITIES

HOBBIES AND OTHER INTERESTS

APPLICANT'S SIGNATURE